6-2-12

Keert:

With greatest respect
and appreciation!

Jestn

THE ACHIEVABLE DREAM:
COLLEGE BOARD LESSONS ON CREATING GREAT SCHOOLS

GOVERNOR GASTON CAPERTON
and Richard Whitmire

ABOUT THE COLLEGE BOARD

The College Board is a mission-driven not-for-profit organization that connects students to college success and opportunity. Founded in 1900, the College Board was created to expand access to higher education. Today, the membership association is made up of over 6,000 of the world's leading educational institutions and is dedicated to promoting excellence and equity in education. Each year, the College Board helps more than seven million students prepare for a successful transition to college through programs and services in college readiness and college success — including the SAT® and the Advanced Placement Program®. The organization also serves the education community through research and advocacy on behalf of students, educators and schools.

For further information, visit www.collegeboard.org.

In all of its book publishing activities, the College Board endeavors to present the works of authors who are well qualified to write with authority on the subject at hand and to present accurate and timely information. However, the opinions, interpretations and conclusions of the authors are their own and do not necessarily represent those of the College Board; nothing contained herein should be assumed to represent an official position of the College Board or any of its members.

© 2012 The College Board. College Board, Advanced Placement Program, AP, SAT, SpringBoard and the acorn logo are registered trademarks of the College Board. AP Potential is a trademark owned by the College Board. PSAT/NMSQT is a registered trademark of the College Board and National Merit Scholarship Corporation. All other products and services may be trademarks of their respective owners. Visit the College Board on the Web: www.collegeboard.org.

Library of Congress Control Number: 2012938734

ISBN: 978-0-87447-999-7
ISBN: 978-1-4573-0000-4 (ebook)

Printed in the United States of America.

Distributed by Macmillan.

For my wife, Idit Harel Caperton, an education technology innovator, who has been a constant source of knowledge and inspiration.

— Gaston Caperton

For my father, Blanton Whitmire, who always understood that education involves far more than classrooms and diplomas.

— Richard Whitmire

CONTENTS

INTRODUCTION

By Gaston Caperton

I was 8 years old when my parents found out I couldn't read. The call came from my second-grade teacher at J.E. Robins Elementary School, Mrs. Robinson, a professional and dedicated educator who had taken a special interest in her students. My mother answered the phone, completely unprepared for the news she was about to receive, especially since my older sister was an A+ student. School was pretty normal for me up until then, but after that day nothing would be the same.

My parents began to look for explanations and answers. In the late 1940s, learning disabilities weren't much understood and many doctors and teachers weren't sure what to do with me. Some said I was a lost cause — and if it weren't for my mom and dad, I probably would have been. They just refused to believe what some would only whisper: "Gaston's not smart enough; Gaston can't learn; Gaston is stupid." Finally, we went to see a physician who happened to be interested in how eyesight affected learning. The doctor told my father I had the "reversals," which meant if I saw the number 73 it would look like 37.

After a lot of tests and countless appointments with all sorts of doctors and specialists, I finally was diagnosed with dyslexia. Almost immediately after the diagnosis, my parents got to work. There was no whining about my unfortunate situation or their own. Some of my earliest memories are of my father sitting and reading with me at night, bone tired when he got home from work but on a mission to make sure I didn't give up on myself. Every morning, before I would go to school, he would make me sit at the foot of his bed and we'd study the dictionary together. We did 10 or 15 words a day for about two years. As a high-energy kid, this exercise was pretty miserable for me. But my father had a lot of patience. My parents wouldn't accept less than excellence from me, and I worked hard to make good on their expectations.

If you knew my family, you wouldn't have been surprised by my parents' determination. I come from a family of missionaries and explorers, people willing to challenge conventional wisdom and seek out new paths. My mother was born in Japan, where her father was a missionary. My father was born in Slab Fork, W.Va., and left home at age 12 to continue his education at Augusta Military Academy. Then he went on to Virginia Tech to study mining. However, he decided pretty quickly that he didn't want to be in the coal business, and instead moved to New York City to take a job with Western Union.

My mother and father met in New York when my mother, a medical technician living in Richmond, Va., took a trip north to sub for a friend from nursing school. They later returned together to West Virginia, where my father opened an insurance company, and in 1940 I was born in Charleston.

I wish I could say things got easier for me in school after the dyslexia diagnosis. The truth is that school was always tough for me and I had to work harder than most just to keep up. I'm smart, but I was only an average student. As you can imagine, long division and grammar are difficult when numbers and letters get turned around. Despite my academic issues, my mother really wanted me to go to Episcopal High School in Alexandria, Va., where her uncle had been the principal. I knew how important it was to her, so I took the admission tests. I got in, but was told I had to repeat ninth grade. I flunked a couple of courses along the way and had to study during the summers, but in the end I graduated and went off to college.

However, there were certainly moments when it seemed like I wouldn't. One summer day when I was home studying, I saw a letter from the principal. In the letter he told my parents that he didn't think I could do the academic work at Episcopal and that I should not return. My father wrote back, informing him that I was working hard and would return to school to retake the tests I had failed. I did — and passed them all.

The next semester I made what they call the high list (the honor roll). After my name was read at chapel, I recall one teacher putting his arm around me and saying, "Gaston, this is an inspiring day. If you can make the high list, anyone can." My friends and I laughed, but I've always remembered that moment. That was the wrong thing to say to someone who had worked as hard as I had. It was a putdown, plain and simple. I liked this teacher a lot and he was just trying to be funny, but when you're somebody else's idea of a joke it's pretty difficult to see the humor.

ran. The fact that I ran against six people helped. If the race had been one-on-one, I probably would not have come out on top. I ran a positive campaign that didn't talk much about what was wrong with West Virginia, but instead focused on how we could fix it.

I knew it would be a challenging campaign — but thanks to the lessons I learned at a young age I wasn't afraid of hard work. That was important, especially early on when things did not look good. One of the earliest polls showed my support at 2 percent state-wide. A friend of mine pointed out that things could be worse — the margin of error was actually 4 percent, so I should be happy it was at least a positive number. The odds weren't in my favor, but I believed in what I was doing and I worked harder than everyone else in the race. Every day for almost a year I traveled the state in a big van with my name painted on the side, meeting as many West Virginians as I could and trying to convince them that with new leadership, we could pull ourselves out of the economic doldrums and build a better future for our state. Thanks to this positive message, and a little bit of luck, I survived the primary and went on to beat the incumbent governor, Arch Moore, in a close race. Election night 1988 is one of the most special memories of my life, and I was so thankful that my sons were there to share it with me. Making the night even more special was the presence of my father. Even though he would live for only four more months, I knew he helped lay the groundwork for this victory during all those late-night reading sessions so many years earlier. It was his determination that made my success possible.

At the time of my inauguration, West Virginia was in terrible shape. We had a $500 million deficit. Our infrastructure was out of date. And our government was stagnant. This deteriorating state of affairs affected no aspect of public life more than our schools. West Virginia's teachers were some of the lowest paid in the country. Their health care and pension costs were underfunded. School buildings themselves were run down and morale was horrible. Needless to say, there wasn't much learning going on. So I threw myself into the education debates swirling in our state, because I knew education was our way back to prosperity. I made some friends and a few enemies along the way. But the entire time, my focus was on the students and on the state's economic future.

During my eight years as governor we launched the nation's largest basic skills computer program and installed more than

18,000 computers in kindergarten and elementary classrooms. We also formed a partnership with Bell Atlantic-West Virginia to link more than 400 schools to the Internet. A Columbia University study found that West Virginia's use of educational technology led to substantial gains in the math, reading, and language skills of elementary school students. We also invested more than $800 million in modernizing and improving school facilities throughout the state. In all, we built 58 new schools and renovated more than 750 school buildings.

Recognizing the critical role of teachers, we invested millions of dollars into salaries and benefits, bringing West Virginia teacher salaries from 49th in the nation to 31st. We also created the Center for Professional Development to provide teachers with access to the high-quality, relevant, in-service staff development they need and deserve. In addition, we led an effort to promote and reform postsecondary education in West Virginia, pushing for massive higher education reforms. My administration for the first time required colleges and universities to undertake strategic planning that would improve quality, access, focus, use of technology, and openness to change.

By the time I left office in 1997, we had turned West Virginia around. That $500 million deficit had become a $100 million surplus, our school system was on the mend, and our government was finally working for the people instead of the special interests. To this day I find inspiration in the challenges we overcame, and I am incredibly proud that we left the state in much better shape than we found it.

In the last months of my second term, I was asked to come to Harvard University and speak to newly elected members of Congress about education. While there, Harvard invited me to join the university's Institute of Politics. I realized that this was the perfect transition opportunity for me, so I accepted. Soon I wasn't just teaching, I was auditing classes too — religion, history, business, music, and more. After a semester at Harvard, I got an invitation to teach at Columbia University Teachers College, where I ended up teaching for a year and half.

It was during my time at Columbia that I got a call from the College Board asking if I would be interested in interviewing for the president's position. At first, I told them it wasn't for me. Growing up dyslexic doesn't make you want to run a testing company. Tests were rarely my friend. But they kept asking, so I interviewed. I was asked to come back the next week and after the second interview they offered me the job. To the surprise of some, I took it. By that time, I saw the College Board as more than a testing company. It had a lot of potential. For example: When I arrived, the Advanced Placement Program® (AP®) was considered an exclusive program in which only the top students were able to get college credit for taking tests in high school. Just 635,000 students took AP Exams in 1998. Today, that number has risen dramatically, to nearly two million. We recognized that the number of students who could take highly rigorous courses was being limited by the perceptions of educators. There were millions of students out there who were underserved, underrepresented, and understimulated — it was our job to find them, motivate them, and set them on the path to success.

Why the rapid growth? It's not because students all of a sudden became smarter or teachers better trained. It was because we finally recognized the potential of both teachers and students. The capability was always there, it just wasn't being used. In Florida we teamed up with then-Gov. Jeb Bush to administer the PSAT/NMSQT® to every student in the state, so teachers would know which ones were ready for AP courses. Since then, the total number of Florida students taking AP courses has risen from nearly 38,000 to more than 163,000, the number of African American students taking AP has doubled, and the number of Hispanic students has tripled.

My career has taken me from the private sector to government to the world of nonprofits and academia. It has been a remarkable journey. Many great teachers and mentors played a critical role in making me the person I am today, but the most valuable lessons were the ones learned from experience — from succeeding and failing on my own. My dyslexia taught me that everybody has to struggle. I know my struggles were relatively minor, but they taught me the value of hard work and how to deal with disappointment. Perhaps most importantly, I learned to maintain my self-confidence even in difficult times. There are some scars you never fully get rid of. For me, one of those was left early on by the wounding words of those who made me feel unintelligent. Having to prove myself is just something that's always been in me.

....

Around the time I came into office — and years before education became a hot-button national issue — there was a ranking of developed countries based on the number of young people who had earned college degrees. Among 25- to 34-year-olds, the United States ranked third. I remember thinking that wasn't good enough. We used to be No. 1. Today we're ranked 16th — behind Norway; behind Japan; behind South Korea. And if the pattern continues, soon to be behind a host of other nations smart enough to match their understanding of the importance of college completion with the investments that make it possible. At the precise time that the importance of a college degree is increasing, the ability of the United States to compete in the global economy is decreasing.

Looking back, a postsecondary education wasn't always as important as it is today. When I was a high school student in West Virginia, if you didn't go to college your father took you down to the plant or the mill and got you a job. You could make a good salary, buy a house and a car, raise your kids, and retire on a pension with just a high school degree. But those jobs don't exist anymore — and they're not coming back. In the 21st century's global economy, it's not just education, but postsecondary education that is required to compete and succeed. A college education has taken on the same importance as a high school education had in the past. That is why it is critical that all high school students — regardless of race, background, or means — have the opportunity to continue their studies and earn a college degree or certificate. With the economy increasingly dependent on highly educated workers, education, now more than ever, is a crucial link between personal well-being and national strength.

Unfortunately, there are many reasons to be critical of American education: falling test scores; overcrowded schools; too much bureaucracy; and low pay for teachers, to name just a few. But in the pages that follow we will lift the veil on some of the schools that are succeeding against the odds. And I believe that by the time you turn the last page you'll be able to proudly say, "There is hope and opportunity for every American student." These schools are a testament to great leaders and to great teachers, who not only motivate students, but nurture them to excellence; who don't just know their subjects, but know their students inside and out.

The best part of my time at the College Board has been visiting schools like these and meeting students all across the country. Because while it's one thing to read about what great schools are doing, it's another to see them in person and literally feel the energy that makes them so inspiring. The schools profiled here are doing things right, and we can learn valuable lessons from them.

You may notice that this book concentrates mostly on successful schools serving less-advantaged students. We recognize that there are plenty of outstanding private schools and suburban schools serving children from high-income families. But in the years to come, our country will be measured by how we serve the least fortunate among us. It is in our best interest, as a nation, to focus our resources and attention on this growing population of Americans.

You may also notice that, despite my proud West Virginia roots, I decided against profiling any schools or individuals from my home state. It certainly is not because I couldn't find any. It's actually because I have too many examples of excellence and commitment from the many teachers, administrators, and political leaders I have had the pleasure of working with during my career, and who helped develop the major education reform program we implemented during my eight years as governor. Those eight years, and the 13 I have spent at the College Board, have given me a unique and comprehensive point of view for recognizing exceptional work in education — and there truly is much great work going on today in West Virginia. So to all those who lead or have led education reform in West Virginia, as well as to my colleagues at the College Board, I say thank you for not only your support, but also for the knowledge and judgment that have been critical to my job.

So, just who will you read about in the pages ahead?

In the first chapter you will read the story of Bertie Simmons, who came out of retirement at the age of 66 to turn around Houston's Furr High School. In 2011, I visited Furr to award the school one of the College Board's Inspiration Awards, which honor schools that dramatically increase academic rigor for underserved students. I was surprised when I walked in the front door looking for the principal and this rather small woman in her 70s walked up and said, "Hi, I'm Bertie. I'm the principal." I was surprised not just by her stature but by her plain spokenness. But when I walked with her during class change, I saw the real Bertie. Every student who could get close to her gave her a hug or a fist bump. They spoke to her as you would speak to your grandmother, with confidence and warmth. When she spoke at the award ceremony you could have heard a pin drop. In that audience there was a respect and admiration that I've rarely felt in similar circumstances.

Bertie is fearless, and she has a passionate belief that all students can learn. Part of her passion comes from why she came out of retirement. She lost her granddaughter in a tragic accident. Sometimes, tragedies like that diminish people. They lose their zest for life. But Bertie was just the opposite. She used it as an inspiration, and coming out of retirement to become principal of Furr was a way for her to memorialize her granddaughter.

We also tell the story of how Maryland has emerged as the state to turn to when looking for lessons on how to improve schools for all students. Much of the inspiration behind Maryland's success comes from Nancy Grasmick, who recently stepped down as state superintendent of schools. One reason Nancy always had empathy for students with learning challenges stems from her own problems as a child, when a bad reaction to some medication left her fully deaf for a year and hearing impaired for another six months. And while her deafness faded, her interest in the disabled never did. That's why for her first teaching job she chose Baltimore's William S. Baer School for the disabled, where she worked with deaf students.

We'll introduce you to Eduardo Padrón, president of Miami Dade College. The college gave Eduardo a chance to better himself as a young refugee from Cuba when no one else would. He has spent the four decades since giving back to the institution that he now calls "Democracy's College," turning it into an educational, economic, and cultural powerhouse. Enrolling more Hispanics and graduating more black and Hispanic students with associate degrees than any other institution of higher education in the nation, Miami Dade is on the front lines of one of the nation's most significant struggles: students graduating from high school unprepared for college-level work. Three-quarters of Miami Dade students show up in need of at least one remedial course, a scenario that often dooms them to failure and dropping out, but Eduardo and his team have some innovative strategies to engage these young people as well as promising partnerships with area middle and high schools to reduce the need for remediation going forward.

MaryEllen Elia's work in Tampa as schools superintendent is another compelling story we think you need to hear. She took on a big school district that was just kind of going along, put great principals and teachers in place, and raised expectations for everyone. She is practically allergic to anything less than excellence. You can see MaryEllen's fierce determination in her son, who is blind but certainly not disabled. He came to New York to meet with me and walked into the room accompanied by no one but a guide dog. Within minutes I had forgotten he was blind. He talked about hiking the mountains in Austria with the same nonchalance that I tell a story about my walk home from work. There was no embellishment, no sense of him being brave or accomplished. He inherited that from his mother. Not flashy, but strong.

Despite what critics may claim, there are many, many people working to give equal access and opportunity to low-income schools with underserved students; people who are helping students discover the possibilities and potential that they have locked up inside. But far too often, this work goes unrecognized. When you meet the extraordinary educators at these schools, you will immediately see how they transform the lives of their students. You will quickly learn, as I did, that human potential can expand and explode if you have principals and teachers who believe in, and demand the best of, their students. Every day the dedicated men and women at these schools are inspiring students to do well in class, so that one day they'll have the opportunity to do whatever they want in life. Maybe even become a teacher.

Nothing is more special than seeing the excitement in the eyes of the students or hearing the pride in the voices of the teachers. It's just pure positive energy. I firmly believe that we must always keep our focus on what we can and have done to make America's education system better. Anybody can criticize, but it takes special people with special skills and character who have gone out and gotten it done every day to make a difference.

I've seen those breakthroughs in my own family as I watch my wife, Idit, build her business. Idit is an innovator and a visionary. With her two master's degrees and Ph.D. from MIT, she is combining her knowledge of education with her expertise in technology.

Her latest success, The World Wide Workshop, and its flagship product, Globaloria, help students learn to create games of social purpose while working in teams. The program is growing quickly, expanding from West Virginia to Texas, California, and dozens more states. From Idit's work, I've learned how enthusiastically students respond to learning through technology and how quickly a good idea can be implemented in our schools when we work with the right people and the right tools. The World Wide Workshop and Globaloria — along with MaMaMedia, an Internet company Idit founded prior to the workshop — are great examples of how we can use technology and innovation to transform learning and teaching, and take education to a whole new level of student engagement and educator advancement. Living with someone who is on the cutting edge has opened my eyes to the possibilities that arise when big ideas are combined with talented people and hard work.

Just like Idit, the students, teachers, administrators, and policymakers profiled in this book know how important it is to think outside the proverbial box. These educators prove that pockets of our nation's school system function superbly — and not just in the wealthy suburbs. In fact, if most school districts were to follow these examples, the United States could move quickly to reclaim its spot atop the international education rankings.

What we're hoping educators and parents take away from this book is that these schools work because they follow a simple formula: Boost teacher quality, step up the academic rigor of courses, and spread those rigorous courses to more students. AP is not the only way to boost rigor. The International Baccalaureate courses are impressive, as are early college programs now being offered at many high schools that blend high school and college work. While the AP programs get discussed at length in this book — they are what we know best —the point is to get more students ready for academic work beyond high school, whether that be college or training programs. The chapters here go far beyond the work we do at the College Board. For example, one chapter profiles an ideal preschool program; another, a parent engagement program that we think should be adopted by other schools.

We will do our best in the book to stay positive. Thanks to my parents, I've always been a positive person. Despite my dyslexia, they always focused on what I could do and what I could be. They set no limits for me, and I set no limits for myself. That's the spirit

I've tried to bring to the College Board. It's the spirit that fills the hallways and classrooms of successful schools. And it's the spirit of this great country that we are trying to improve all the time.

In my office at the College Board, I have photographs hanging on the wall to remind visitors of what can be accomplished when people stop talking about a problem and actually take action toward a solution. Going around the room, I have photos of a group of students taking sledgehammers to the Berlin Wall; long lines of voters in South Africa's first integrated national election; FDR signing the GI Bill; and Thurgood Marshall emerging victorious from the Supreme Court after *Brown v. Board of Ed.* These historical lessons show what's possible when people step into the arena and strive to do the deeds.

From the Revolution to the Civil War to civil rights, we as a nation have always believed we could be better. Abraham Lincoln stood up for our union because he believed we could be better. He knew that no nation could survive divided against itself, and he made the ultimate sacrifice to ensure that our better angels won the day. FDR carved out the New Deal with the American people because he believed we could be better. He knew it wasn't welfare; it was building a nation. Thurgood Marshall and the NAACP sued the Kansas Board of Ed because they believed we could be better than separate but equal. It is in that context that we write this book — as a call to action to make education a national priority, because we know we can be better once again. A great deal of time has been spent over the years identifying the problems with our education system. But what has defined the American spirit throughout our history is not our ability to pinpoint a problem, but our capacity to take action — to pay any price and bear any burden when called to service.

During the most challenging times in our history, education has transformed our nation and set us apart from the rest of the world. After World War II, we passed the GI Bill — educating a generation of veterans and helping to create the great American middle class. A decade later, Sputnik spurred investment in primary and secondary education — leading to the great technological advancements of the 20th century, from satellite communications to the Internet. As we make our way out of the Great Recession, in an increasingly competitive global economy, our nation faces a similar challenge.

I dedicate this book to the remarkable educators I have had the pleasure to work with over many years — the people who get up every day and go to work because they believe our country can be better. They believe that if we demand more from students and provide them with the support and guidance they need, young people can do better — because with hard work and an education, every student can do great things. Through the dedication of these inspiring educators, we come to realize our potential. I thank these education leaders for being in the arena and for working so hard to push open the doors of higher learning for everyone. Their dedication reminds me of a quote from one of my favorite presidents, Teddy Roosevelt — a quote that hangs on the wall in my office beneath a picture of my sons and me taken the night I was elected governor:

"It is not the critic who counts; not the man who points out how the strong man stumbles, or where the doer of deeds could have done them better. The credit belongs to the man who is actually in the arena, whose face is marred by dust and sweat and blood...who does actually strive to do the deeds; who knows great enthusiasms, [and] great devotions; who spends himself in a worthy cause; who at the best knows in the end the triumph of high achievement, and who at the worst, if he fails, at least fails while daring greatly, so that his place shall never be with those cold and timid souls who neither know victory nor defeat."

Part 1

ACHIEVING GREAT LEADERS

Bertie Simmons came out of retirement at age 66 to take over
Houston's Furr High School.

Chapter 1

AN OUTSTANDING PRINCIPAL

The first thing you need to know about Bertie Simmons is that "Bertie" is not a nickname. That's her given name. Oddly, once you meet her, "Bertie" seems like an entirely appropriate name. How could her parents have known? The next thing you need to know about Bertie Simmons is that when we visited her (in October 2011) she was 77 years old and running a very smooth Houston high school that draws students facing some of life's steepest challenges. One newspaper profile of Furr High School dubbed it "Homeless High." And that's just the regular high school. She also created a separate high school on the same campus that takes in dropouts still trying for a diploma. She didn't bother going through many bureaucratic hoops to launch the dropouts school — it just needed to be done, so she did it. The last thing you need to know about Bertie Simmons is that she came out of retirement at age 66 to take on this assignment. Doesn't everyone take on near-impossible challenges at that age?

Now, on to the Bertie Simmons story.

Simmons grew up in tiny Chatham, La., a town where at that time few left for college. Not only was Simmons determined to leave for college, but she aspired to be a dancer. "I used to lie in the backyard at night under the stars and think about the day I would get outside those walls and go to Broadway, where I would be a dancer." Simmons did get out of Chatham for college, but only as far as Natchitoches, La., to attend Northwestern State

University. "I was in the dance class there and was looking in the mirror at all those long legs and girls throwing them up, and my legs were like two feet long. I looked at my legs compared to their legs and realized I had to get out of dancing. I decided instead to be a choreographer, and I was pretty good at it."

While in college, Simmons suffered from a freak medical occurrence — a stroke. "I got up one morning and I couldn't move the left side of my body and I was slurring my speech. I thought, 'What on earth is happening? I'm so young.'" The effects of the stroke passed (and she suffered no more strokes through age 77), but she decided to change her major once again, to dance education. Upon graduation, however, the jobs available were in traditional education, so she began a long career as a teacher in Louisiana elementary, middle, and high schools. While teaching in Kinder, La., she learned the difference between coaching and playing. Because she had been a standout basketball player in high school, she ended up taking over the girls basketball team. But playing has little to do with coaching. "I'd see all those other coaches out there talking to their players and I didn't know what to say to my players, so I'd tell them, 'Just go out and put it in the hoop.' I think we won three games that year and lost 30, so I lost my job. That was a big failure for me. I had no idea how to coach."

Teaching, however, became a love. When she moved to south Louisiana, she taught math and English to high school students whose first language was French. "We would just dive in together, and we would all learn together with a lot of hands-on activities. I loved watching the lights come on in their eyes as they learned. It just did something for me that nothing else had ever done. I realized that teaching is probably the most important job in the whole world."

Arriving in Houston

In 1956, marriage brought Simmons to Houston, where urban teaching was an abrupt reality change. At that time, Houston schools were segregated. Integration, however, was under way. After teaching 10 years, Simmons, who is white, became a "teaching strategist" in all-black schools as Houston Independent School District (HISD) went through integration and designed urban magnet schools intended to help with the process. "That was an exciting time, and it was done peacefully," she said. "But one of the things we did I didn't feel good about was we took the good African American teachers and put them into white schools, while the teaching spots in the black schools often went to brand new white teachers from the East Coast." The older white Houston teachers, it was thought, would never adjust to teaching in black schools. Simmons's job as a teaching strategist was to help the young white teachers. But there was no escaping the reality that the best teachers, white and black, ended up in the white schools.

Setbacks

Next, Simmons became a principal for five years, then a regional superintendent. Several years later, however, her career got derailed — the result of a confrontation over the appointment of a principal she didn't approve of, she said. Her demotion and transfer cut short all the school integration work she had been doing. "We had really brought the African American and Hispanic families together," Simmons recalled. "We would have parent conferences with 2,000 people participating. I was kind of shocked that this happened, because I always had this idealistic approach in believing that all people wanted what was best for kids. That was a learning experience. I had never been ill since that stroke, but I came down with pneumonia — the worst kind of pneumonia you can imagine. My immune system completely shut down. And I realized it was not just because I was losing a position that mattered, but I was losing the dream I had worked so long for, and the people I had grown to love."

Eventually, with a new superintendent (and a lot of sharp elbows thrown in a closed-door board session), Simmons regained her former position. But six years later Simmons again found herself in a confrontation, this time over how a cheating investigation was handled by the central office, she said. Simmons resigned — abruptly. That resignation at age 60, she assumed, would be her retirement, at least from Houston schools. For a time, that seemed to hold, as Simmons worked as a consultant and then with a kids-advocacy nonprofit.

Then everything changed dramatically. In the winter of 1999, Simmons went skiing in New Mexico with her granddaughter, Ashley. "She was 16, in 10th grade, a scholar — she was taking all AP classes — and loved all people. She just had such a good heart." That winter had been warm, which produced poor, wet snow. "Her ski hit a root and it catapulted her out of her skis and her head hit a tree. She died instantly." The death was horrific to the entire family. "That was just the most devastating thing that could happen to you in your life."

At the time, Simmons and Ashley were collaborating on a book about generational leadership, and Simmons wasn't sure she wanted to finish. But she persevered. As part of the book research, Simmons visited a Houston doctor who worked with AIDS patients. In a discussion about death, Simmons was struck by the physician's candor with patients. For those with a chance to recover, he would encourage them to fight. "Don't give up!" he'd tell them. But for those certain to die, he had another message. "For those patients, he would say, 'You need to let go. It's okay; you're going to be at peace.'" From that, Simmons took away a personal lesson. "I realized I didn't need to give up. I needed to keep going. And that's what made me finish the book." (The book, illustrated by Ashley's father, was published in 2000.[1])

The Comeback Call

In the spring of 2000, just as Simmons was struggling with all these issues, she got a call from a superintendent at HISD: Please come out of retirement and take over as principal at Furr High School. Simmons said no — twice — and then reconsidered. "I remembered that Ashley had always said she wanted to make the world a better place for all people. I thought I might be able to make Furr a better place since Ashley would not be able to accomplish her dream." The superintendent asked Simmons to take over for three months to see what she could do to turn the school around. Simmons was fully aware of Furr's reputation, with its rock-bottom academic standards and gang violence. But, she reasoned, "I can take anything for three months."

At the time, nobody expected much from Simmons. The Furr teachers, accustomed to doing what they wished regardless of the embarrassing academic outcomes, expected only one thing from Simmons, a hasty and welcomed departure. To the students — all minorities bused in from Houston's poorest neighborhoods, especially the Maxey Road and Fleming projects (most of them well aware they were considered HISD's castoffs) — this white-haired grandmother named Bertie must have seemed like an apparition from an alternative universe.

Simmons was introduced to the staff on a Friday. The following Monday, her first day on the job, was a shocker. All the beautiful furniture she had seen in her office on Friday had disappeared. In its place was an old desk brought in from the trash bin. "The drawers didn't even open." Even worse was the replacement chair the teachers had found. "It was one of those old chairs with no arms and just a little padded back, which was broken and flopped over with the stuffing hanging out." An office that had been clean on the Friday before was now littered with cigarette butts — "They knew I didn't like smoking" — and reeking of smoke. Simmons had to run the entire school by herself that first week, which was spring break; the rest of the office staff hadn't shown up. "They were sending me a message that they did not want me here. I thought to myself, 'I am too old for this. I have to be crazy to be doing this.'"

The Gamble

The reception from the students was just as dramatic. "One kid threw another through a plate-glass window. I walked in and there was blood shooting from his throat. There were kids with boom boxes walking up and down the halls, going into classrooms. And the students would be sitting on top of the tables or desks, eating, doing whatever."

At that time, the police department had identified 14 different gangs operating on school grounds. "They were all fighting and throwing garbage cans; it was just awful." One day after a riot on campus, an assistant principal identified 32 gang members and recommended they be sent to an alternative school. "I said no, because if we sent those kids to the alternative school they would come back behaving the same way. I decided to break the rule. I thought, they could send me to the house [Houston schools jargon for the central office], or better yet, to the home. So I called them all in and asked what it would take to bring peace into their lives and the school. And they started talking. Nobody had ever listened to them before; nobody had valued their ideas. Nobody thought they knew anything." During the discussion, they complained that authorities were always trying to fool them. None of the students, for example, actually thought the attacks of 9/11 took place. That was just something President Bush made up, they told Simmons. "They hated George Bush because he had been their governor. They thought he was only for the rich people, that he didn't care for poor people."

Then Simmons shocked them with an offer: "If you sign a contract with me that you will stop fighting for the rest of the school year, I will take you to New York City and show you Ground Zero." The young men were both surprised and wary. None had been on an airplane and they were scared of flying. They asked if Simmons would drive them. "I told them, 'I'm not driving a bunch of thugs to New York. I'm old; we're going to fly.'" Finally, the gang members signed off.

After the contract got signed, the fighting stopped and the fundraising started. Not surprisingly, the corporate donors who often supported school activities were wary about sponsoring a New York outing for gang leaders. "I couldn't get a penny from anyone," Simmons said. Finally, an informal fundraising network materialized (helped by comedian Jon Stewart's mother, who had worked as a consultant at Furr) and pulled in enough money from around the country to launch the trip in the spring of 2003.

Again, the boys pleaded with Simmons to drive. "Here they were, with tattoos everywhere, just tough people, and they were scared to fly." To ease their fears, Simmons persuaded Continental Airlines to allow the students to visit the Houston airport and tour a Continental jet. Still, flying remained their biggest fear. "They all asked to sit next to me, and I told them I couldn't save them. If the plane goes down, we're all going down." The trip, which included a Broadway show, the United Nations, and the Statue of Liberty, went beautifully. "I didn't have one minute of trouble." At Ground Zero, she noticed some of the students were praying in the nearby church. "I asked if they were praying for the people who lost their families, and they said they were praying the plane wouldn't crash on the way back."

Back at Furr, Simmons was learning more about the violence the school had experienced. The school had Cholos, Crips, Fed-X, and MS-13, she said, along with neighborhood gangs such as The Little Reds, Northside, and Denver Harbor. The police officers assigned to the school treated the students as if they were deadly

Furr students flock to Simmons as she walks the hallways.

gang suspects, she said. "The police had gang task force members here, and I saw them slamming kids around. They would throw them to the ground and put a knee to their backs. One day I saw one of my students, a good student, accidentally bump one of the task force members. They grabbed the student and threw him up against a brick wall. I couldn't stand that."

Simmons had the gang task force removed. "When I did that one of the task force members came in and screamed at me that the building would implode and they would not send anybody to help me; I would be on my own. It never did implode. It got better and better. I hired police officers who have my philosophy, those who believed that if you treat people with respect and don't take away their dignity, they will mostly do what you want them to do."

What About the Teachers?

Turning around the corps of teachers at Furr was a challenge more difficult than curbing gangs. In those days, it was extremely difficult for a principal to remove low-performing or problematic teachers. For years, Furr had earned a reputation as a teacher dumping ground. The best teachers left, their spots filled by teachers transferred there by principals happy to part with them.

For nearly seven years, Simmons waged a battle on two fronts, working with the best teachers to plan the future of Furr and "counseling out" the teachers who didn't belong there. "They thought I was going to die, but I kept living." Over the next seven years, she counseled out nearly 70 teachers, persuading them they would be better off elsewhere or even out of education.

Convincing the teachers to perform as a team was a huge challenge. The fourth summer after arriving, Simmons arranged a trip for 21 teachers to Estes Park in Colorado. Before leaving, everyone took personality tests and then was grouped based on those tests. The idea was to teach everyone to work collaboratively, even with very different people. "We climbed Old Man Mountain and got to the top just as the sun was going down. It was gorgeous, but then we realized we had to hike down in the dark and depend on one another." Another day they went rock climbing. Again, personality tests determined who belayed whom with ropes. "I asked my biggest nemesis, who had given me a hard time, to belay me. He questioned the wisdom of the request: 'You know I don't

like you.' I answered: 'But you wouldn't let me die, would you?'"
The Estes Park trip proved to be a turning point for the staff she
needed on board to take Furr in a better direction.

Finally Turning to Academics

When Simmons arrived at Furr, the school offered no AP classes.
Because of the long struggle to turn around the teaching staff
there, the AP offerings didn't arrive until 2007, and that was just
a handful. By 2011, however, 62 percent of the 735 students were
taking AP courses and another 16 percent were taking pre-AP
courses. "This was really a big stretch for us because most of our
parents speak only Spanish. We not only had to convince the kids
that rigor was important, we had to convince the parents. I met
individually with 351 parents and their students last year and
told them it wasn't enough to graduate from high school and go to
college. You have to be successful in college. They bought into it."

Most Furr students still earn 1s or 2s (a score of 3 or higher is
considered the equivalent of passing a college-level class), but the
dramatic ramping up of academic rigor was enough to earn Furr
an Inspiration Award from the College Board, which included
a check for $25,000. Said HISD Superintendent Terry Grier at
the award ceremony: "We've made it our goal to become the
best school district in the country. The way to get there is to
increase the number of students taking more rigorous college-
level courses, to have an effective teacher in every classroom
and an outstanding principal leading every school. Furr is a good
example of the type of turnaround that can happen when you
bring all those factors together."

Anyone experienced in touring inner-city schools can
immediately recognize a school where there's no fear and the
students and teachers respect one another. That calmness
and respect was apparent while touring Furr. Simmons was in
constant demand for hugs from the students. She never passed
a male student with low-riding pants without stopping to make
sure they got hitched up — requests met more with humor than
resistance. She's witty. She's grandmotherly. She's just, well, full
of piss and vinegar. Bertie Simmons is every student's favorite
grownup — someone you want to escort to her car at night to
make sure she makes it safely, which the students do. As for the

academics, a visitor walking unannounced into classrooms saw that actual teaching and learning was taking place, something that for many years was almost unknown. For Homeless High, that's an impressive accomplishment.[2]

In hindsight, it is clear that Simmons, steeled by brutal professional and personal reality checks, was ideally positioned to take on the fierce challenges she found at Furr. Hostility was met with equanimity. Resistance was met with persistence. She proved to be the antithesis of the Hollywood-glorified Joe Clark, the New Jersey principal who seized control of his school with fierce discipline, landing him both a movie and a *Time* cover wielding a baseball bat. Simmons was the diminutive, charming, gutsy, plain-speaking grandmother who, in the end, nobody could resist and everyone respected.

Endnotes

1. Bertie Austin Simmons and Tarrant Fendley, *Wind for New Wings: A Message from the Leaders of Today to the Leaders of the New Millennium* (Houston, TX: Houston Printing Services, 2000).

2. The decision to profile a principal such as Bertie Simmons warrants a footnote. How many principals are there out there with her unique personal history and drive? Not many. The turnaround Simmons brought to Furr borders on the "cult of personality" warning heard from education experts: Don't count on finding enough teachers and principals with those unique talents to fuel widespread turnarounds of struggling schools. Those warnings are apt. And yet Simmons did what any promising principal must do. She was relentless in her goal of fielding a corps of teachers who believed that her students at "Homeless High" could learn. She knew exactly when and how to push the accelerator on academic rigor. And she listened to students unaccustomed to being listened to. That turned a toxic school culture into a family school culture. The challenge for HISD will come in replacing a principal such as Simmons, a challenge that worries Simmons as well.

Preston Smith is a constant presence in Rocketship classes.

Chapter 2

VISIONARY SCHOOL BUILDERS

Even before the Santa Clara County (Calif.) school board members gaveled themselves into session, it was clear this was going to be no ordinary meeting. Steady streams of Latino parents, most with kids in tow, had filled the huge meeting hall. These were people who mostly went unnoticed in the high-tech corridors of San Jose. They hang your drywall, clean your hotel rooms, and wash your restaurant dishes. To accommodate the crowds, school board officials opened up an adjoining room, then another, then another after that. In the end, nearly 700 people braved the infamous Silicon Valley evening rush hour. Many were turned away when the school board ran out of rooms to open. They all showed up in support of the last item on the agenda: Should the board approve three more Rocketship Education charter schools?

Little girls, their heads not even clearing those of the seated adults, paced the meeting room walkways with signs, some with English lettering on one side, Spanish on the other:

More Rocketships/More Kids to College

College Class of 2030

Everyone Deserves an 892 API School[1]

Then the parents testified, about half relying on a translator. "I don't have a lot of money," said one mother. "All I have is my encouragement that my kids go to college." Said another mother, "Rocketship gives me the feeling that everyone is family." A third mother: "A lot of families want to move their kids to Rocketship, but there is a long waiting list." A mother with two girls at Rocketship charters said, "Rocketship is giving us parents hope. They believe in our kids. You have the ability to be champions tonight."

After seeing Rocketship parents in action that night, the conventional wisdom that Spanish-speaking parents rarely become school activists suddenly looked outdated. At the end of the hearing, the board members turned aside objections to the expansion — from the California Teachers Association, from some of the school superintendents in the county, and even from the board's own staff — and voted 7–0 to permit three more Rocketship charters. Truly, this was no ordinary school board meeting, and Rocketship is no ordinary charter school network.

Charter School History

The school innovators who launched the first charter schools roughly 20 years ago had two goals in mind: They wanted their publicly funded but independently run schools to be incubators of innovation, and they wanted to offer better school choices to families in poor neighborhoods. Freed of the bureaucracies of regular school districts, these experimental schools would pioneer instructional models so successful that traditional schools would then adopt the same practices, they reasoned. In addition, they would level the playing field for students from low-income families who, unlike their middle-class counterparts, lacked the option of buying their way into better schools by moving to pricier neighborhoods.

If the charter school movement were judged by popularity, it would walk away a clear winner: By 2011, more than two million children would be enrolled in charter schools. Measured by the original goals, however, the movement comes up short. For the most part, traditional school systems viewed even the best charters as unwelcome competitors and rarely tried to imitate their innovations. Worse, most one-of-a-kind charter schools, dubbed "mom and pop" charters, proved to be no better than regular neighborhood schools, unworthy of imitation.[2] True, parents liked having a choice, but from an academic achievement perspective the choice didn't always lead to better academic outcomes for their children.

Although on average charter schools don't stand out from regular schools, there are important exceptions. The big development in the charter school movement was the emergence of charter networks that blended powerful and consistent teaching innovations to close the achievement gap. These charter management organizations, such as KIPP (Knowledge Is Power Program), Uncommon Schools, Achievement First, Aspire, YES Prep, and Green Dot, produced extraordinary schools in some of the nation's toughest neighborhoods, leading them to be dubbed "no excuses" charters: Poverty and poor parenting should not be an excuse, their leaders vowed. KIPP, the best known of this group, got its start in 1994. By the end of 2011, KIPP operated 109 schools in 20 states and the District of Columbia, educating 32,000 students.

Despite their successes — as seen in a dramatically favorable light in the documentary *Waiting for "Superman"* — these high-performing charters had limitations in their ability to grow quickly. Teacher burnout was a problem, as was finding enough talented principals to lead new schools. In addition, with very few exceptions these elite charters shied away from doing what beleaguered urban school chiefs (and Education Secretary Arne Duncan) most wanted them to do, which was take over regular public schools that were failing.[3] Also slowing down the no-excuses charters was the fundraising required to supplement what the schools received in per-student public funding.

The Rocketship Model

Then, in 2007, a new charter model emerged in California's Silicon Valley: Rocketship Education, which served low-income Latino children, almost all of whom came from homes where Spanish is the first or only language. These K–5 schools blended no-excuses teaching techniques with the computerized Learning Lab, where students spent roughly a quarter of the day. Using programs such as DreamBox Learning to teach math, Rocketship schools helped students strengthen their basic skills in the lab, thus giving teachers more freedom to use classroom time to push beyond the basics and encourage the kind of "higher order" learning skills common to middle-class schools.

By 2011, the Rocketship schools, co-founded by former Silicon Valley entrepreneur John Danner and teacher/school founder Preston Smith, remained modest in breadth: five schools serving nearly 2,500 students in the San Jose area.[4] Regardless, the Rocketship charters began drawing national attention. The test score gains turned in by Rocketship students were striking, but just as striking was the innovative blended model. By relying on the Learning Lab, Rocketship was able to both grow and thrive on the extremely modest per-student budget granted by California. Rocketship schools serve 500 students with just 16 teachers, compared with the roughly 21 teachers needed for a traditional school or charter school of the same size. The smaller staff allows for higher pay: Currently, Rocketship teachers make 20 percent more than teachers in the neighboring county school districts. In 2014, the scheduled pay moves to 50 percent above the neighboring schools. Two years after that, the plan is to pay teachers double the average surrounding school district salary, or slightly over $100,000.

The higher pay helps compensate for the longer hours, one of the drivers of teacher burnout at other elite charter schools. But that's only part of the plan to avoid burnout. The goal is for the Learning Lab to take care of the basics, which are less stimulating to teach, allowing Rocketship teachers to focus their classroom time on the more challenging, and more interesting, instructional tasks. Rocketship's promotion strategies are also designed to combat burnout. Unlike some charters, which favor hiring Teach For America (TFA) graduates after they have proven themselves during the two-year obligatory experience, Rocketship almost exclusively hires beginning TFA recruits and conducts its own training and professional development. The most promising teachers — perhaps only one or two years out of college — get channeled into a leadership track. That gives Rocketship a deep pool of homegrown talent available for expansion schools. Just as important, Rocketship teachers see the opportunity for quick advancement. Why peel out of teaching to go to law school or Wall Street when the future appears bright in education as they earn $100,000-a-year salaries?

The final innovation was Rocketship's approach to parental involvement. At most schools, both charters and traditional, parental involvement is a head nodder. *Of course* you want parental involvement. That's *so* important. What teachers and administrators want most from parents is effective parenting, especially when it comes to backing school practices and showing up for parent-encouraged activities such as back-to-school nights. That's enough — no more. In truth, the high-performing charters that design long school days Mondays through Fridays and part work days on Saturdays reap a benefit that is understood but rarely spoken about: As a result of that schedule, their students spend less time in toxic home neighborhoods. The school becomes the de facto family, thus raising the odds that students will get an education that can lead to a productive life.[5] At Rocketship, parental involvement is far more than a head nod. From the perspective of Danner and Smith, the more intense the parental involvement, the better. And as witnessed at the November school board meeting, active parental involvement is part of the Rocketship expansion plan.

Rocketship's Record

None of these innovations would mean much unless the students at Rocketship were succeeding in the classroom. Overall, Rocketship is the highest-performing low-income elementary school system in California. At Rocketship's first school, Mateo Sheedy Elementary, nearly all the students are minorities and low income and yet 71 percent scored proficient or better on California's reading tests in 2011; in math, 84 percent. Now compare that to nearby Gardner Elementary, a traditional elementary operated by San Jose Unified School District with mirror demographics. At Gardner, only 40 percent of the students scored that high in reading, and 62 percent in math. Also within San Jose Unified is Willow Glen Elementary, located in a less-poor neighborhood where only half the students are minority and only half live in poverty. At Willow Glen, 68 percent of the students scored at proficient or above in reading, and 73 percent in math.

One more comparison within Santa Clara County: Just 19 miles west, in the shadow of Stanford University in far wealthier Palo Alto, is Ohlone Elementary School, which has a primarily white and Asian student population. At this school, only 13 percent of the students come from poor families. At Ohlone, 84 percent of the students in 2011 were proficient in reading, 83 percent in math — roughly the same as what was achieved by the low-income Latino students at Mateo Sheedy.

Have John Danner and Preston Smith invented charter schools version 2.0?

The true test for Rocketship will come as the group expands beyond Silicon Valley and its proven base of succeeding with low-income Latino students. But it appears that Danner and Smith have created a charter school model that, to borrow the vernacular of social policy entrepreneurs, is uniquely "disruptive" and therefore likely to drive change among both charter and traditional schools. Many charter and traditional schools are also experimenting with blended learning. But when the entire Rocketship package — everything from instructional practices to teacher and leadership development — gets weighed, the evidence suggests that Rocketship may be the high-performing charter school network most capable of scaling up quickly.

"We created Rocketship to have an impact," said Danner, who, after selling his Internet company and deciding that education was his passion, taught in Nashville public schools for three years and helped found a KIPP charter school there. "We think of it as the second generation of charters. The first generation was to prove that the achievement gap could be closed, so you had the KIPPs, YES Preps, Uncommon Schools, and Achievement Firsts. The big goal for that phase was to make the point that any low-income child could achieve at a level similar to any high-income child, and I think they really made that point."

Expansion Plans

Rocketship's goal, however, is different. In Nashville, Danner saw no evidence that the leaders of the traditional Nashville schools were interested in adopting KIPP's educational practices, thus limiting the impact a KIPP school could have. "If you are going to have an impact, you have to set yourself up so that you can grow in a way that you solve the problem — not count on others to solve the problem for you," said Danner. "If the problem in San Jose, for example, is that there are 15,000 students in the elementary schools that are below grade level, instead of creating one or three or five Rocketship schools and then hoping that the districts would figure out what we're doing, we basically built an engine that would let us figure out how to create all 30 schools that needed to be created."

John Danner brings his Silicon Valley expertise to charter schools.

Creating those 30 schools in Santa Clara County, a huge county with multiple school districts, is what brought Danner and his team once again before the Santa Clara County Board of Education on Dec. 14, 2011. The "ask" was 20 more charter schools, which would bring the total number of Rocketship schools in the county to 30. That request was opposed by the teachers unions and many of the superintendents who operate districts within the county. Every child enrolled in a Rocketship charter is one less child entering their school system.[6] Once again, Rocketship parents flooded the hearing room. "Our students do not have time for the public education system to improve," said one parent. In the end, the board voted to approve the 20 schools. Explained one board member: "We are at a crossroads here, and we have a chance to take the road that will change everything. I cannot in good conscience ask parents to wait."[7]

Asking for 20 more charter schools struck many as audacious. Actually, that request was modest when compared to Rocketship's broader expansion plans. The overarching goal laid down by Danner and Smith is to eliminate the racial/economic achievement gaps — and that's not just a head nod. There are 13,000 failing schools in the country, say Danner and Smith, so to help districts eliminate the gap, Rocketship must reach the stage where it can open 10 schools a year.

Among educators — even among operators of high-performing charter schools — hearing those twin goals might lead to raised eyebrows, or worse. Who do they think they are? To place Rocketship's ambition into perspective, consider that the highly regarded KIPP organization, backed by a phalanx of deep-pocketed philanthropists and some of the most creative education innovators in the country, managed to open "only" 109 schools in its first 17 years. But within the very tight Rocketship organization, the goal of eventually being large enough to affect the entire public education system is taken very seriously. For the near term, their plan (ranging from certain to maybe, depending on multiple approval processes) includes: rapid expansion in Santa Clara County; eight schools in Milwaukee, with the first opening in the fall of 2013; another eight in New Orleans; and a gradual expansion in the Bay Area, with schools in San Francisco and East Palo Alto. The most important near-term goal is to demonstrate that they can replicate Rocketship in a city outside of California.

Every decision at a Rocketship school gets filtered through the expansion plan, says Aylon Samouha, Rocketship chief schools officer. For example, a charter school group that aspires to reach 100 schools can work from a long-range plan that factors in annual fundraising of $1,000 or even $2,000 per student. But at a scale of opening 10 new schools a year, that goal would be unthinkable. "There's just not enough money in either government or philanthropy for that," said Samouha. Solution: Design your schools to survive on just the state per-student funding, no more.

Teacher quality is another example. At a small scale, it is possible to find teachers who for at least a couple of years will work endless hours before burning themselves out and leaving. They can be replaced. "It may not be morally great to do that, but from a cold-hearted perspective you can keep burning out teachers and rotating more in. It is a big pain and it takes a lot of energy and resources, but it is not a deal killer," said Samouha, who knows something about recruiting high-quality, motivated teachers. Before coming to Rocketship, Samouha was in charge of teacher development at Teach For America. "But when you're opening 10 new schools in a city each year, that *is* a deal killer. There just won't be enough teachers to replace the ones you burn through, so that is not an option."

Rocketship Staffers

Rocketship's unique approach to human capital can be seen in the personal stories of teachers such as Sharon Kim, a Korean American woman born and raised in Dallas. In her early years as a Cornell University undergraduate, Kim never considered teaching. But then she took a couple of education courses, got inspired by listening to author Jonathan Kozol speak, and discovered Teach For America. Law school or TFA? Kim chose TFA. After a five-week TFA crash course in teaching, she got recruited by Rocketship and ended up at Mateo Sheedy Elementary School. There, she spent another month in training that covered everything from how to handle Rocketship's reading and math programs to understanding the unique culture of the mostly Mexican American families who send their children to Mateo Sheedy.

In August of 2009, only a few months after graduating from Cornell, Kim began her Rocketship career teaching four classes of kindergarten math, 30 kids per class, most of whom didn't speak much English and few of whom had been to preschool. This meant they lacked what educators call "school readiness skills" — a term that covers everything from basic academic skills to how to sit at a desk, raise your hand, or use a school bathroom. "The first few days were extremely difficult. … It really rocked my world. I had to learn all their names, but within the first hour they ripped up the name tags and threw them away." But with the help of the Learning Lab, professional development, and coaching (at times, Rocketship mentors, called academic deans, stand in the back of the room and coach wirelessly to earbud-wearing teachers), Kim caught on to the Rocketship system and her students responded.

"She got some exceptional results her first year," said Samouha, "and continued to get exceptional results in her second year." As a result, in only her second year Kim became an "emerging leader" in the Rocketship system, which triggered training preparation for a leadership spot. In the 2011 school year, Kim became an assistant principal at another Rocketship school, the last step before taking over a school. Although Kim proved to be an exceptional teacher — few new Rocketship teachers get tapped for the leadership pipeline in their second year of teaching — what is more striking is the rapid promotion system. Three years out of Cornell, Kim is an assistant principal.

To Danner, teachers such as Kim prove Rocketship's theory about talent development. "There are two myths about Teach For America," said Danner. "One myth is that a first-year TFA corps member is a kind of tax on the system, that they are going to do poorly. The second myth is that they are going to leave after two years to go to law school, business school, medical school, or whatever." In many cases, Danner said, those graduate school plans are more desired by the parents than the TFA-er.

Thus the Rocketship formula: Teach For America delivers bright, motivated, partially trained candidates. Rocketship then develops them into effective first-year teachers (relying heavily on Doug Lemov's teaching techniques: see Chapter 4). In the last step, the most promising teachers get promoted quickly into a three-year leadership training track, giving young teachers truly interested in education the option of a challenging, fast-moving career they can choose over graduate school. "I mean, if I'm a school principal by age 26, I would feel good compared to my friends who are off being lawyers and bankers," said Danner. "Yes, they may get paid a little more, but I've got a way better mission and I'm increasing my impact."

The Restart Offer

Another edgy part of the Rocketship expansion plan is offering traditional school districts "restart" options. As with most of the other higher-performing charter organization leaders, Danner and Smith won't agree to take over management of a failing district school.[8] But Rocketship *will* offer restarts. An example: Rocketship agrees to lease a vacant school building near that failing school, or even within a school closed because it failed to improve. Families within that school zone get first priority to "opt in" to the new Rocketship school. If seats are still available, the balance of the school comes from families outside that school zone whose parents want their children to attend a Rocketship school. In-zone parents not wanting to send their children to the Rocketship school would have the option to enroll their children in the closest traditional elementary school. "Opting in is pretty important to us. We don't just sit in our offices. We do home visits and a bunch of outreach. At the end of the day we don't want to force people in. If they haven't bought in, they should go to another school."

In theory, the local school district benefits by having a new, high-performing school take in students who had been in a failing school. Plus, the Rocketship school would be part of the district rather than a charter "competitor" taking away their students. That's the theory. The reality promises to play out differently. To date, many superintendents and principals have viewed charters such as Rocketship as unwelcome competitors likely to skim off the most motivated parents and trigger losses in state per-pupil funding.[9] Some parents worry that the arrival of Rocketship would lead to the closing of their neighborhood schools, which they often value regardless of the academic outcomes. Finally, teachers union leaders know that even if Rocketship schools are folded into an existing school district, they would maintain an independent staffing system, which means the unions are likely to oppose the expansions.[10]

The counter-balancing forces in this political dynamic, Danner believes, are parents demanding better schools, the kind of pressure witnessed at the Santa Clara County school board hearing when the Rocketship expansion plans were debated. Plus, Danner is counting on school boards starting to acknowledge the impressive academic gains made so far by Rocketship schools with the most at-risk students. "There should be a different charter-school authorizing process for charter systems with track records than for those with no track record. ... Let's just agree on what the quality of the school needs to be, and then make the approval cycle a lot more efficient." Danner and Smith have a streamlined argument to make before school boards, mayors, and superintendents: The academic progress made among the high-poverty Rocketship students is solid, Rocketship teachers are well paid, and Rocketship parents are not only happy but also motivated to see the group expand. What's not to like?

"If you can double student performance and double teacher pay," said Danner, "the existing system is going to have to figure out what to do about it."

Endnotes

1. The Academic Performance Index (API) is a single number from 200 to 1000 that reflects a school's overall performance level on California's standardized assessments. APIs can be compared across schools statewide and are also used to compare a school with 100 other schools that have similar challenges and opportunities. California's API for grades two through six in 2011 was 808. Rocketship's Mateo Sheedy, with an API of 892, is in the top 20 percent of elementary schools statewide and the top 1 percent of low-income elementary schools statewide. The median API of its similar schools was 770, about 125 points below Mateo Sheedy.

2. Center for Research on Educational Outcomes, *Multiple Choice: Charter School Performance in 16 States* (Stanford, CA: Stanford University, 2009). 37 percent of charters do worse than regular public schools, about 17 percent do better.

3. There are exceptions, such as Green Dot Public Schools taking over management of failing schools in Los Angeles.

4. Danner, who holds a master's degree in electrical engineering from Stanford University, founded and served as CEO of NetGravity, an Internet advertising software company. Danner took NetGravity public and sold the company to Doubleclick in October 1999. Smith, a former Teach For America corps member, helped found a new public school in the San Jose area.

5. Interestingly, a similar attitude emerges at elite private schools: Please, parents, these students are under enough pressure. Leave the educating to us.

6. Their public argument before the county board, however, was that Rocketship should seek approval from individual school districts (where, for economic reasons, approval would be far less likely).

7. Sharon Noguchi, "Santa Clara County School Board Votes to Approve 20 New Rocketship Charter Schools," *San Jose Mercury News*, December 15, 2011.

8. To Danner and Smith, the Rocketship system is all or nothing, which means a clean sweep of teachers, administrators — everyone — and parents agreeing to have their children enter the Rocketship world.

9. School superintendents are right: Reductions in the student population trigger reductions in state per-pupil funding. Marguerite Roza, a senior scholar from the Center on Reinventing Public Education at the University of Washington, argues that the real issue is that most school districts do a poor job of expanding and contracting (especially contracting) with enrollment changes, regardless of the reason for the change. What most school districts consider "fixed costs," such as buses and the size of the teaching staff, are expenditures that private industry would not consider fixed, she says.

10. After the November 2011 Santa Clara County school board hearing where members voted 7–0 to approve three more Rocketship charters, board President Joseph DiSalvo wrote a blog entry about being "verbally attacked" by union members, who contend the board's approval violated the law, a contention likely to be settled in lawsuits. DiSalvo, a retired educator, is a former grievance chair, vice president, and president of his local chapter of the California Teachers Association. Wrote DiSalvo: "...the California Teachers Association wants to put up legal roadblocks against doing what is proper for our underserved children. CTA's interest appears to be in keeping the status quo. The status quo has not done right by low-income children for decades. Thirty-one percent of [Santa Clara County] Latinos drop out of school before completing high school."

MaryEllen Elia has almost singlehandedly transformed Hillsborough County Public Schools.

Chapter 3

AN EXCEPTIONAL SUPERINTENDENT

Few would dispute that the nation's urban educators face challenges that each year only seem to get tougher as poverty becomes more concentrated and language barriers get more complicated. Conventional wisdom holds that all urban districts perform at roughly the same level of effectiveness, which would be somewhere near the bottom. But that's not true. Some urban districts produce far better results despite the challenges. Students in California's Long Beach Unified School District (profiled in Chapter 11), for example, have long benefited from living in a district that has found smarter ways to educate its students, most of whom face the same disadvantages seen among students in other urban areas. More recently, educators in North Carolina's Charlotte-Mecklenburg Schools have been winning praise for reforms that are clearly working for students.

The metric for comparing urban schools is a ranking by the federal Department of Education that comes out only every two years — a relatively obscure index (though it's anything but obscure to those running urban school districts, who consider it their Academy Awards) called TUDA, for Trial Urban District Assessment. The federal government samples students in fewer than two dozen urban districts in reading, math, science, and writing and then posts the results. For those who lead urban districts, the day the TUDA results get posted is worthy of a drum roll. On Dec. 7, 2011, the department unveiled its latest TUDA comparisons, this time adding a new urban district to its list: Hillsborough County Public Schools. The newcomer looked impressive, rivaling Charlotte-Mecklenburg, the 2011 winner of the prestigious Broad Prize for Urban Education. In reading scores, Hillsborough fourth-graders led all 21 participating districts. Minority and low-income students from Hillsborough were standouts.

Hillsborough? Doesn't sound urban.

Actually, the district, located in Tampa, Fla., is the nation's eighth largest. Among its 193,000 students, 22 percent are African American and 29 percent are Hispanic. For nearly a quarter of the students, English is the second language. And nearly 6 of every 10 students qualify for free or reduced-price meals. Until recently, Hillsborough wasn't on anyone's best-of list. But that has changed quickly. Today, educators curious about seeing cutting-edge teaching evaluations in action — evaluations that weren't forced on teachers but rather created with their guidance — need to travel to Tampa. And for anyone curious about observing some of the nation's most ambitious attempts to prepare students not traditionally considered college material to take higher-level courses likely to propel them into college, the place to book a trip to is Tampa.

Most of the changes at Hillsborough can be traced back to a single individual, Superintendent MaryEllen Elia, a schools chief easy to underestimate. She looks like everyone's favorite aunt, her politeness reflects her childhood upbringing, and her speech is free of the terse verbiage of the firebrand school reformers. But underestimating Elia (pronounced EEL-eee-ah) would be a mistake.

Growing Up Sheltered

When Elia was a small child growing up in upstate New York in the 1950s, she was told she could be anything she wanted, as long as that anything was a nurse or educator. That's just how things were at that time, especially in tiny Lewiston, N.Y., where Elia was sent to all-girls Stella Niagara Seminary, graduating in a class of 12. That was followed by an all-girls Catholic college in Buffalo, N.Y., where she was a history major. "I loved history. … I'm a firm believer that you learn from errors, either your errors or those of others. You have to have a feel for history so that you can use that past experience to make decisions about what we should be doing in our world."

In Elia's world at that time, it quickly became clear that something was awry. While in college she had volunteered as a tutor in inner-city Buffalo, her first exposure to the world outside her small-town life and sheltered Catholic schools. "It was the first time I really saw the difference in neighborhoods, the wide gap in poverty." It made a lasting impression. In declaring a major, Elia's father had set a clear bar: "MaryEllen, whatever you do when you come out of college, you've got to be able to get a job." That seemed like a reasonable request, so Elia added education as a minor to her history major.

After spending her junior year traveling abroad in Europe, seeing her European history studies come to life, Elia returned to college and embarked on her student teaching at a large suburban school, Sweet Home High School in Amherst, N.Y., just outside Buffalo. Elia taught American history, world history, and a packed course called "crucial issues," a senior-year elective. That last course, where students undertook independent research and made presentations to the class, got Elia excited about teaching as a career and also planted ideas for how she would eventually structure schools in Tampa. "It was an eye-opening experience. I got to realize that students are some of the best teachers of their peers — that whole concept of open discussion and questioning by other people who don't know as much about the topic. It was a great experience for the kids to have."

Learning to Love Teaching

Elia's successful student teaching led to a job offer from Sweet Home to teach history, which she accepted. After taking maternity leave for a year in 1974, she returned to Sweet Home to find that another teacher had been assigned to her favorite class, AP European History. Because of the lack of interest, however, the class was no longer offered. So Elia made an offer to the principal: Allow me to teach this course for free for one year to see if I can build a following. The principal agreed. "Some of my colleagues were not pleased with that because I was going against the contract by teaching an extra period with no salary for it," she said. "But I really wanted that course to make it." And it did, even with seniors usually plagued by the indifference of senioritis. "Getting these seniors working and thinking about the things that had happened in history turned into one of those experiences you never forget." The following year, close to 20 students signed up for the course.

Recognizing Reading Problems

In 1979, Elia's career took an unusual step that would shape the rest of her career path as an educator. She earned a second master's degree, which was unnecessary for meeting school district salary "step" requirements. This master's was in teaching reading. "People told me I really should get a doctorate instead, but I thought that's really not what my kids need in school. I did the second master's because my students couldn't read in high school, and you have to be able to read to get a feel for history." The problem was not basic reading skills but rather the challenge of reading complex texts, such as primary source material needed for advanced history courses.

The problem Elia recognized at the time — reading deficiencies among high school students, even those coming from a middle-class background — put her nearly 20 years ahead of most educators. Today, many high schools are just beginning to teach reading skills in the upper grades, a task that secondary teachers have traditionally left to elementary school teachers. The reading problem, says Elia, arose from the "reading wars" of those days, where some students got shifted to whole language instruction that skipped over the phonemic instruction many students need to sound out word constructions. "Some teachers might be using whole language, others phonemic awareness. There was such variance in how teachers were taught to teach reading." Many of her students received an incoherent mashup of the two very different schools of reading instruction, she said, leaving them lacking in reading fluency in high school, just as they were about to enter college. "I really focused on what you could do with older students who didn't have good reading instruction."

The Move to Florida

Elia taught at Sweet Home until 1986, when her husband, a businessman, got a job offer in Florida and they moved to Tampa. There, her reading background proved to be a useful fit for educators beginning to recognize reading deficiencies among their older students. Elia was assigned to a high school as a reading specialist. Her task was to convince teachers in all subjects to inject reading instruction into their daily courses. It wasn't always an easy sell. "You would get this attitude: 'I'm a history teacher; I don't teach reading. That's not my job.'" Eventually, however, she won over most of the teachers — even the physical education teachers: "I taught them how to get their kids to understand the graphs and charts that are part of football and baseball. I tried to make it relevant to their subject area. For coaches, this became their rainy day activity."

In 1989, Elia became reading supervisor for all secondary students in Hillsborough schools, which led to a series of other assignments at the district office, including designing magnet schools that were part of the district's court-ordered desegregation plan. Not everyone believed magnets would work. "At one point, one assistant superintendent told another: 'I'll bet you a steak dinner at Bern's Steak House [a well-known Tampa restaurant] that you will never get white kids to get on a bus and travel to the inner city to go to school.'" That administrator lost the bet. "We filled those schools. I had kids clamoring to get on buses."

Learning How to Boost Rigor

When Elia served as general director for high schools, she moved quickly to both expand the number of students taking AP courses and improve the training for AP teachers. At the time, only a select few students took AP courses (less than 10 percent) and many of them earned scores too low to qualify for college credit. "I told the principals and the teachers union that any AP teacher has to go to summer training. That was really radical." And she made it clear that teachers who didn't want to reach out to more students needed to move aside. That, also, didn't go over well. "The principals didn't want to change people who had been in the subject area for years. But I told the principals that if the teachers weren't accepting of more challenging students and weren't doing a good job, they either needed to fix themselves or try something else."

To force the process, Elia set up the PSAT/NMSQT test, given in ninth grade, as an automatic pipeline into AP courses. Students achieving a promising score on the test were scheduled for an AP class. Thus, skeptical guidance counselors and teachers were partially removed from the decision process.

Predictable pushback on this new policy came from teachers and principals worried about sinking scores on the AP Exams. In the past, that was how they measured their success. "I told them the new policy had two thrusts: You have to have more kids get into AP classes and you have to have the teachers see their roles as teaching all the kids in the class, not just the 'smart' ones." Less predictable pushback came from parents asking that their children be removed from the more challenging classes: "The parents would call and say they can't live with their kids who are complaining so much about the additional work — please take them out." Elia told her principals to hold the line against the parents. "If you have a kid who is not in a course that he should be taking because he is smart enough to do well in that class and you're letting him take a pass, that's not the right thing to do."

Elia's message to the principals: If the parents persist, have them call me. A few did. One parent called to insist on removing his son from an AP European History class. After learning the boy aspired to attend the University of Florida, the state's most selective public university, Elia warned the father that dropping the class would hurt his chances of getting admitted. Still, the father insisted. "I said, 'Okay, but I need for you to sign a form saying you understand your son has the ability to do this class but you don't want him to take the class.'" The father signed the form and removed his son. But the message got through. The next year, his junior year, the student took three AP courses. In his senior year, he took three more. "My philosophy is that we are the educators. It is our responsibility to tell parents and students that this is what you should be doing. It is our field. It is like a doctor telling you to do something. You do it."

In 2005, the superintendent's position in Hillsborough opened up. Despite being a long-shot candidate (the departing superintendent recommended someone more senior), Elia decided to go for it. "I told my husband that I really thought I could do this job the best, that I had really strong values about what should happen here. He said, 'MaryEllen, if you don't put your name in, you will never have a chance. What's the worst that can happen?'" After a three-month search-and-interview process involving multiple candidates, the board chose Elia, mostly because of her aggressive push to raise academic rigor. "With the board I was very open about my determination to have more kids have access to

MaryEllen Elia spends time in the lab with some of her district's students.

higher-level course work. Even if the students don't do well on the exam, the exposure gets them thinking differently, reading many more types of articles and texts. They get better at synthesizing all that." Given the demographics of the district — high minority and high poverty — that was an edgy position to take. But the board picked Elia, thus launching one of the nation's most compelling experiments in remaking an urban school district.

How Elia's System Works: Leto High School

Jessica Maloney, 17, is the type of student Elia had in mind when she launched her campaign to spread academic rigor. Jessica is a senior at Leto High School, a school that once was the top academic school in Tampa, attended then by nearly all white, middle-class students. Over the years, the school's demographics have changed dramatically. Today, Leto is 85 percent minority, almost all Hispanic, and is one of the highest-poverty schools in the county (more than 80 percent of the students are eligible for subsidized lunches). It's the kind of school where some teachers get asked: Do you feel safe teaching there? (They do. In fact, at period changes the hallways at Leto have a family-like feel to them.)

Jessica is a vivacious African American senior, the baby among seven siblings. When interviewed, her eyes sparkle and a smile never vanishes. Her mother is a day care teacher; her father, a construction worker. Jessica has striking educational aspirations. She wants to attend the very selective University of Florida, and she wants to major in either premed or pharmacy. If she succeeds, Jessica will probably be the first in her family to graduate from a four-year college.

What gives her confidence is her strong interest in math and science and the ambitious course-taking at Leto. Each of her four years there she has taken AP courses. To an outsider, what's intriguing about Jessica is that she has never scored a 3 or above on any of her AP Exams, the level students need to reach to qualify for college credit (the top score is 5). In elite private schools, students scoring anything less than a 4 on an AP Exam might feel somewhat embarrassed. But Jessica is anything but embarrassed — nor are her teachers. Presenting college-level material to students with no college-going experience in their families is part of the aggressive AP program at Leto.

"A score of 1 or 2 only means that you are not ready for college credit," said Eric Bergholm, who oversees the district's effort to ramp up the number of students taking high-rigor classes. "That student still took the course and most likely received a decent grade and got the benefit of a rigorous curriculum. ... A score of 1 means you are ready for high school; you're rocking it. That's fine. They are in high school. A 2 is actually pretty good. That means you are perched to receive college credit. You can't fail an AP Exam. A score less than 3 just means you didn't receive college credit." (Although some of Hillsborough's AP students never earn college credit, there is no district in the nation that has achieved a larger increase since 2008 in the number of students earning AP Exam scores of 3 or higher.)

Debbie Prill, who chairs the English department at Leto, agrees with the strategy of expanding AP access. "Jessica was still subjected to that level of rigor. She knows what it's going to be like in a college class and that is going to pay off. Jessica will get through college. She won't be one of those kids who starts off and never graduates." Jessica has no regrets about her ambitious AP schedule. "When I go to college and take those classes again I think I'll be well prepared and do really well in them."

Using SpringBoard®

To prepare Leto students to take college-level courses that traditionally are taken only by middle-class white students, Hillsborough relies on SpringBoard®. Starting in the fall of 2009, all 73 middle and high schools in the district launched the College Board–designed program that changes not only what gets taught, but how it is taught. No longer do students sit quietly and listen to the teacher. With SpringBoard, students learn from one another (the power of student-to-student learning was something Elia observed in her first year of teaching in upstate New York), which means a lot more discussion among students than most teachers are accustomed to tolerating. With SpringBoard, simplistic quizzes about just-read texts disappear. What counts are critical thinking skills, especially those expressed through writing — just as the students will need in a college-level class, whether they take that class in high school as an AP offering or in college. Either way, the students get prepared for college.

On the day we visited Leto, English teacher Giselda Montenegro was using SpringBoard to explore the themes in Edgar Allan Poe's *The Cask of Amontillado* with her ninth-graders. But instead of the traditional discussion, the students were building a storyboard of Poe's masterpiece, as though they were movie directors. Instead of looking at a single theme, the students explored multiple angles, just as a movie director would do.

Prior to SpringBoard, students would have read the Poe story, settled on a single theme, and answered questions at the end of the chapter, said Alice Wuckovich, coordinator for SpringBoard language arts programs. What Montenegro was teaching was the art of "back mapping," where students look for more than one perspective on a piece such as *The Cask of Amontillado*. They are also asked to reflect on the learning tools that led them to their perspectives. It's something akin to the difference between an onion and a peeled onion. "A director wants to manipulate your feelings. You first have to examine how you feel about a character. If you are creating a storyboard, what would you put in the shot to tell the scene — angle, lighting, sound — to manipulate the audience?" The point of this more complex exercise is simple: In two years, many of these students will be taking AP English, a class where they will face essay questions that demand high-level critical thinking. For many middle-class students whose parents are college graduates, these skills come almost naturally. At Leto, those skills are taught, preferably two years in advance. Scoring above a 3 on an AP Exam would be nice, but the real goal lies in preparing these students to be the first in their families to graduate from college.

The Elia-inspired strategies of channeling more students into higher-rigor courses, a push that included reorienting student counseling toward college readiness, appears to be working:

— The number of juniors who took the PSAT/NMSQT rose from 46 percent in 2007-08 to 87 percent in 2010-11.

— The number of juniors taking the SAT® increased from 39 percent in 2007-08 to 65 percent in 2009-10.

— The number of finalists for the National Merit, National Achievements and National Hispanic awards reached a district high of 95 students in 2010-11, an increase of 25 percent over three years.

— Hillsborough received several awards for having the nation's largest increase in the number of students earning a 3 or better on AP Exams from 2008 to 2010. Despite the surge in the number of students taking AP Exams, the district maintained its average for earned scores.

Part 2

DEVELOPING GREAT TEACHERS

Lauren Catlett runs her classrooms with rhythm and precision.

Chapter 4

BUILDING BETTER TEACHERS

Michelle Shearer, the 2011 National Teacher of the Year, realized she was destined to teach while she was an undergraduate at Princeton University and promptly switched her major from premed to chemistry. The Maryland science teacher holds dual certifications in science and special education. Earlier in her career, Shearer taught for four years at the Maryland School for the Deaf, carrying out all instruction in American Sign Language. At that school, she was the first teacher to offer AP Chemistry. Her advice to other teachers: "The very first thing you have to do every day when you wake up is ask yourself, 'Do I really believe that all students can learn?' One of the reasons I put so many pictures of students on my walls is it helps me remember all those faces of students who can learn and do learn."[1]

Anyone reading through the accomplishments and credentials of recent state and national Teachers of the Year would come away profoundly impressed. These teachers are extraordinary. One national Teacher of the Year, from Iowa, rivals some professors in her academic achievements: multiple honor societies, National Board Certified, a winner of the Promising Teacher Award from the Iowa Council of Teachers of English. But she's no academic stiff. Her lessons often incorporate songs and Facebook. "When I look in a classroom, I see a story in every learner, unique and yearning to be read," she said.

The state teaching champs are hardly slouches, either. One Florida Teacher of the Year took pride in her hands-on learning style, at times dressing up as a pirate or Albert Einstein to help drive home the lesson. The résumé of one New Jersey Teacher of the Year includes surveying reefs in San Salvador, supervising an archaeological project in Jordan, mapping Native American sites in the West, and exploring in Mongolia, Belize, Egypt, and Morocco.

Conventional wisdom holds that these were born teachers, the kind all parents dream their children will land. Isn't that the story behind all great teachers? At the school level, that's often the belief. Some people are just gifted with a personality destined to command a class. But where do we find more born teachers to inspire our students? Those teachers, of course, will always be in short supply. Given what education researchers tell us about teacher quality, that is unfortunate. Students lucky enough to draw three highly effective teachers — the kind of teachers who might at least be in the running for a Teacher of the Year nomination — soar in learning while their less fortunate counterparts, the students drawing three bad teachers in a row, are pushed to the back of the academic pack (see Chapter 5). Stanford economist Eric Hanushek drives it home with this conclusion: Students with a teacher ranking in the top 5 percent walk away with a year and a half of learning, while students stuck with a teacher from the weakest 5 percent walk away with only half a year of learning.

On the importance of drawing great teachers, parents need little convincing. In the academically aggressive suburban schools, moms learn the subtle and politically acceptable ways of signaling to a principal that their child would do better with this teacher rather than that teacher. Everyone knows how that game works. The problem with the game, of course, is there aren't enough born teachers to go around.

But what if great teachers could be made rather than born?

Any parent visiting True North Troy Preparatory in Troy, N.Y., just a few miles from Albany, can get a glimpse into what may be a prototype for a great teacher "factory" of the future. Nothing fancy about this school: From the outside, it looks like a glorified sheet metal factory. No lush soccer fields. No running tracks. No room for such luxuries. The Conrail yard is so close to the back of the school that the engineers maneuvering their slow-moving locomotives through the yard can peer through the windows and read what teachers have written on the blackboard.

But this charter school, serving nearly all minority and high-poverty children, has something special going for it. Its founder and master teacher, Doug Lemov, author of *Teach Like a Champion: 49 Techniques that Put Students on the Path to College,*[2] provides more than inspiration to the teachers. Lemov, managing director of Uncommon Schools, which are among the highest-performing charter schools in the nation, tracked down truly effective teachers from around the country, studied their strategies, and put it all into a book that teachers here refer to as the "taxonomy" — the 49 techniques that allow any teacher, introvert or extrovert, to walk into a class of 30 fifth-graders, all of them first-year students at Troy Prep, all of them coming from regular Troy public schools where most have fallen one or two grades behind in learning in classrooms where unruly behavior was the norm, and be highly effective teachers. From the first day. Even if they aren't born teachers. Sound impossible? Pretty much, until you see it in action.

Mastering the Techniques

Let's enter the classroom of Lauren Catlett, 31, who this day is teaching fifth-grade writing. The class is scheduled to run 70 minutes. This is only her third year of teaching, and yet, according to Lemov, Catlett became effective during her first year on the job and has only improved as she infused the 49 techniques with her own personality. And it has nothing to do with being a born teacher, or garnering academic prizes, or earning two certifications, or mapping reefs in San Salvador. Her success comes from two sources: the desire to be a successful teacher and her dedication to embracing Lemov's taxonomy as a powerful teaching tool and adapting it to her own personality.

....

11 a.m. — Preparation

Catlett enters a classroom, which is being used by reading teacher Nikki Frame, 10 minutes early to write lessons on the blackboard. In any other school, this would be considered a rude interruption and most likely would disrupt the teaching flow. It would simply never happen. But at Troy Prep, the students pay no attention as Catlett writes fresh instructions on the board and sharpens pencils. The teachers here are accustomed to almost drenching degrees of collaboration with other teachers. And the students and teachers are accustomed to constant observations by classroom visitors. They barely notice. At one point, Frame draws Catlett into the teaching lesson, which is anything but distracting. The attention from two teachers delights the students. By doing this preclass preparation, Catlett wastes not even a minute of instruction time.

11:09 a.m. — The Greeting (Technique 41: Thresholds)

At Troy Prep, classroom greetings are a three-step process called "thresholds." The teacher from the previous class delivers the students, all quiet in a straight line, to Catlett's classroom door. Catlett stands outside and greets them, one at a time. Step one: Shake hands with a firm grip. Step two: Establish direct eye contact. Step three: Say "good morning" to each student. In Catlett's case, she mixes up her greetings between English, Spanish, French, and other languages. Often, she'll weave in a personal comment as well. "The point is to get started on the right foot. A fresh start, no matter what happened in the class before. You build a relationship."

11:10 a.m. — Learning Capitalizations (Technique 22: Cold Calling)

A worksheet lays out the rules for capitalization, and Catlett challenges students to pick out the sentences with correct and incorrect capitalizations: "The recipe in *The Art of Cooking Well* says to add Black Beans to the soup." (Hint: Don't capitalize foods.)

How to make sure students are absorbing the lesson? Cold calling, Lemov argues, is a way of ensuring that all students stay engaged. "If students see you frequently and reliably calling on classmates who don't have their hands raised, they will come to expect it and prepare for it. ... Cold calling increases speed in both the terms of your pacing (the illusion of speed) and the rate at which you can cover material (real speed)."

Catlett cold calls Jarahn: "What's your answer?" Jarahn answers … incorrectly.

Catlett: "If you agree with Jarahn, give me two snaps. If you disagree, two stomps." The class answer was a mix of stomps and snaps. Not a good sign. Clearly, there's still a lot of misunderstanding about whether "black beans" should be capitalized.

Catlett decides against dragging out the mixed opinions and cold calls Moses, suspecting he would get it right. He does. "I just wanted to get to the heart of the lesson." Catlett then reinforces the right answer with an easy way to remember the capitalization rules. "Frank saw a silly walrus jogging." Each beginning letter stands for things that should never be capitalized: food, seasons, sports, weather, and jobs. Before moving on, Catlett then circles back to Jarahn, making sure he knows the rules. He does.

11:24 a.m. — Technique 32: "SLANT!"

Borrowed from the KIPP charter schools, SLANT stands for: Sit up. Listen. Ask and answer questions. Nod your head. Track the speaker. For Catlett, the message is simpler. SLANT means sitting up straight, elbows tucked in, hands folded on the desk, eyes on the speaker.

Catlett calls SLANT so often, about every five minutes, that she barely remembers saying it. To Catlett, and her students, it has become a reflex. "It's a way of making sure that everyone is listening and compliant," she said. It works. Every time Catlett calls out SLANT, students sit up straight and fold their fingers.

11:25 a.m. — Technique 36: 100 Percent and Technique 23: Call and Response

Nothing short of 100 percent of the students following the directions and authority of the teacher will do, asserts Lemov, who concedes that sounds both authoritarian and impossible to achieve. In most urban school classrooms, the percentage of those riveted entirely on what the teacher is asking ranges from zero to half. Writes Lemov: "… 100 percent compliance may sound terrifying and draconian: a power-hungry plan for a battle of wills or the blueprint for an obedience-obsessed classroom where little but grinding discipline is achieved." In practice, however, teachers can carry this out in warm, positive, and near-invisible ways.

On this day, Catlett has moved to the "brain race" portion of the worksheet, a list of 14 sentences, most of them needing editing for capitalizations. Catlett truly treats it as if it were a race, something akin to seeing a professional football team go through a no-huddle offense. Catlett, a marathon runner, uses her runner's watch to keep the exercise under two minutes: "You should be on number two by now."

Two minutes expire and Catlett shifts to call and response:

Catlett: "Check …"

Class: "… or change." Clearly, the class loves shouting out a response. Everyone responds. "Check … or change," a familiar call and response, simply means it is time to check or change your answers.

Catlett: "Pencils up." Prepsters know it is time to pick up their pencils, poising them over their worksheets. It's a way to control pencils (which in traditional classrooms have a way of ending up skittering across the floor, twirled between fingers, or tapped on desks). Here, the pencils stay in the desk slots until the "pencils up" command is given. And they get returned in unison, as well.

Pencil control, however, is only part of the strategy. Every student sees every other student engaged. It's 100 percent engagement, enforced by group consensus. Students see other students complying, so they comply. Yes, cynics could call it "control." But it appears to work.

Catlett: "Track!" This is another technique aimed at getting 100 percent compliance. Catlett says it every time she calls on a student: "Track Moses." That means all eyes have to be on Moses.

"Tracking" is quick and efficient, especially compared to the traditional ways of getting a class to pay attention, such as asking students to raise their hands as a signal that they have stopped talking. Look at the hands-raised command from the student's perspective: "If I don't raise my hand, can I keep talking? If I raise my hand from the elbow, is that okay? If I wave my hand wildly in the air, is that okay?" Not only is time wasted as the teacher waits for all students to raise their hands, but students learn that partial compliance is acceptable. And partial compliance is not 100 percent compliance — the rate Lemov insists on to achieve 100 percent of the students learning the lesson.

11:31 a.m. — Technique 4: Format Matters

Catlett: "RTQ." She will repeat that command many times during these 70 minutes, and every child knows what that means: Restate the question. Students often answer questions in fragments. One, two, maybe three words. The answer may be right, but it's not in a complete sentence.

Lemov, who observed part of Catlett's class that day, singled out her insistence on teaching students to use complete sentences. "You notice that one of the things we see about Lauren is her passion about writing, especially using complete sentences," he said. "The complete sentence is the battering ram that knocks down the door to college." Catlett produces those complete-sentence answers by the frequent use of RTQ. All the students know that means: Don't bother answering unless you have framed your thoughts in complete sentences.

Another advantage of restating the answer in a complete sentence, Catlett said, is that it produces "sticky" learning. Students will hear it repeated. And the more "at bats" students have hearing or speaking, the more likely the lesson will stick.

RTQ, which at times makes the class sound like a Jeopardy game, also gives the teacher a chance to correct slang or nonstandard English. "Axed," for example, will always be restated by the teacher as "asked." Or, "she got" will be restated as "she has." That's a sensitive issue that Lemov takes on directly. "People who are raised in the middle class, or aspirational class, know the expectation is that they will go to college. So they might speak a dialect at home, but they know that when they are in the workplace or at school, there is a language of opportunity. It's what you speak when you go to a job interview, when you walk into a college classroom. It's a gift to kids to have them practice speaking that way."

11:40 a.m. — Technique 49: Normalize the Error

Getting answers wrong is part of learning. First you get it wrong, then you get it right. It's a normal process, so why not "normalize" getting answers wrong?

Catlett calls on Asiaonna to tell the rest of the class which words in a sentence on the worksheet should be capitalized. Asiaonna proceeds (mistakenly) to tell the class that every word should be capitalized.

Catlett barely responds, instead calling on another student, who gets it right. Then she has the class guess what "the prepster" (she is careful to not identify Asiaonna, even though the other students know who made the mistake) might have been thinking. Several students raise their hands and suggest the prepster might have thought the entire sentence was a book title. Yes, Asiaonna agrees, that was it. Now she gets it — as does the rest of the class. All part of the normal process of learning.

11:45 a.m. — Technique 1: No Opt Out and Technique 3: Stretch It

Asiaonna had quickly realized her error, but Catlett had moved swiftly by her, eliciting the right answer from others. But under "No Opt Out," a student is never allowed to say "I don't know" and avoid further attention.

Lemov: "Reluctant students quickly come to recognize that 'I don't know' is the Rosetta stone of work avoidance. Many teachers simply don't know how to respond. The result is a strong incentive for students to say 'I don't know' when asked a question."

In this case, Asiaonna wasn't trying to dodge the question. Regardless, Catlett brought the question back to her. Catlett draws on the "Stretch It" technique, where getting to the right answer is used as a peg to expand the lesson.

Catlett: "How do we know it's not a book title?"

Student: "Because it's not in italics." (The "stretch" in this case is introducing the use of italics.)

Catlett: "Asiaonna: How do we know it's not a book title?"

Asiaonna: "It's not in italics."

11:50 a.m. — Technique 46: The J-Factor

J, as in "joy," was everywhere in Catlett's class that day. It started with Catlett handing the students a "sticky" way of remembering to put lots of descriptive detail into their writing.

Catlett: "Your reader is a *moron*" (and therefore needs lots of details).

Catlett: "What is your reader?"

Class: "A *moron!*" Clearly, they love it. The call and response gets repeated.

Catlett then deliberately makes up a sentence devoid of any descriptive detail.

Catlett: "What is your teacher?"

Class: "Miss Catlett is a *moron!*" At this point, every student is 100 percent engaged and laughing. They can't believe they are being allowed to call their teacher a moron. Pure joy.

Then, things get even more joyful. At Troy Prep, students get "scholar dollars" that can be redeemed for supplies or, better yet, brandished as tickets to lunchtime in the gym, where students with a surplus of scholar dollars win privileges such as basketball after lunch. Today, Catlett shakes things up a bit by offering "meat scholar dollars," all pegged to the need to add meat — descriptive words — to sentences. The most descriptive writers among the students — those, for example, who had far more to say about their favorite restaurant food than a simple "good" — got meat scholar dollars. Each dollar was in the shape of a T-bone steak with the words: "Your reader will never go hungry." This was beyond joy — the meat scholar dollars became instant collector's items.

12:13 p.m. — Technique 20: Exit Ticket

Catlett: "All right, prepsters, you have three minutes to complete your exit ticket."

Exit tickets are a final at bat, a last chance to go over, once again, the lessons on capitalization and descriptive writing. It's nothing more than a simple question with a written response that gets collected by Catlett and read that night. Did they really understand the lesson?

Lemov: "Not only will this establish a productive expectation about daily completed work for students, but it will ensure that you always check for understanding in a way that provides you with strong data and critical insights. What percentage of your students got it right? What mistake did those who got it wrong make? Why, in looking back at their errors, did they make that mistake?"

12:17 p.m. — Technique 30: Tight Transitions

At Troy Prep and other high-performing urban schools, teaching resembles choreography. Before the class started, Catlett avoided wasting precious instruction minutes by appearing in her classroom 10 minutes early to write on the board (despite the fact that another class was under way in the room). At the end of the class, she saved precious instruction minutes by ensuring that the exit tickets were passed out as quickly as possible. It's a precision-guided event that requires practice. Average time spent passing out papers: 12 seconds.

Final moment of class — Technique 46: The J-Factor

As the students begin to move to their next class, single file, they hear a rival class doing chants.

Rival class: "We are the best! You know it! We have to confess!"

Catlett: "Class, shall we respond?"

Catlett's class: "We are the best! You know it! We have to confess!" Everyone weighs in with the shouted chant, smiles all around.

....

Catlett came late to teaching. Teaching first interested her while she was working on a master's degree in fine arts at American University in Washington, D.C. For an assignment in a literary journalism class, she profiled a KIPP charter school, another high-performing charter group similar to Uncommon Schools. The seed was planted. After moving to Albany to be with her husband, Catlett began looking for new work and heard about Troy Prep opening. "I was so excited. I wrote the boldest cover letter of my life, saying I believe in data and results," she said. "I wanted to make it clear that I understood the mission. Then I got the interview and the rest is history."

The first year of teaching, said Catlett, was the hardest year of her life. Seeing the teaching techniques in action (Lemov's book comes with a DVD showing the teachers at work) is different from creating that same magic in your own classroom. "These are techniques that every teacher applies differently," said Lemov. "When she first tried them, they didn't sound like her." Catlett agrees. "I spent the next year working just as hard, if not harder, than my first year to write material that reflected my personality and allowed me to engage my kids. I really had to think about how I wanted the taxonomy to look in my classroom. ... It wasn't a magical transformation. Applying the taxonomy well takes a lot of planning and hard work." Much of her success comes from the fast pacing described above — pacing that comes from meticulous planning. Said Lemov after watching Catlett teach, "She makes a grammar lesson exciting."

Every day, Catlett and the other teachers here demonstrate that poverty (and several years of bad schooling before the students arrive here) does not have to equal destiny. The test scores from this new school back that up. Nearly 95 percent of the students here qualify for free or reduced-price lunches — a poverty rate higher than any of the surrounding school districts — and yet in 2011, every sixth-grader at Troy Prep scored at the proficient or advanced level in math; two-thirds scored that high in reading and writing skills.

But the Troy Prep teachers have a huge advantage. Each teacher was reinforcing exactly the same teaching techniques. Students arrived at Catlett's door already well indoctrinated in the 49 teaching strategies. The more compelling question is whether a teacher in a traditional, less successful urban school (such as the schools the Troy prepsters attended in their earlier grades) could use those techniques in isolation. Lemov answers yes — with caveats:

"Most of our evidence comes from Teach For America. Let's say you don't have an administration that backs you. You don't have a system of other teachers who are walking around talking the same language. Yes, you can do much of this on an island [the term used for any teacher trying to carry this out in 'isolation'], but you have to do things to remind kids that it is different in your classroom. It is more effective and much more enjoyable if you do it with a team of people doing the same thing. But I think you can make a demonstrable difference on an island."

The most hopeful sign that teachers everywhere believe the techniques in Lemov's book can work for them: As of the fall of 2011, sales of *Teach Like a Champion* reached nearly 400,000 copies.

Endnotes

1. Liana Heitin, "National Teacher of the Year Sees Abilities, Not Disabilities," *Education Week,* May 3, 2011.

2. Jossey-Bass, 2010.

Dean Mayme Hostetter, working with Relay student Alonte Johnson, is among those with the daunting yet enviable job of determining what it takes to create a great teacher.

Chapter 5

OVERHAULING EDUCATION SCHOOLS

With jeans and heavy messenger bags, the sleepy charges trudging up the stairs and filing into classrooms could almost pass for students at this high school in Manhattan's Flatiron district if not for the paper coffee cups they are clutching and the fact that today is Saturday. In room 407, an English classroom during the week, Mitch Brenner is looking for a volunteer. "Do I have a brave teacher?" he asks. Most of the 15 off-duty teachers are rookies, and only one of them raises a hand. "Bryon, thank you very much. I appreciate that. Bryon, come on up," says Brenner, a congenial guy in a red sweater-vest to which he has affixed a University of Wisconsin pin as the Badgers advance toward the Big Ten championship today.

Bryon Eagon, 23, is wearing a Wisconsin T-shirt underneath a navy cardigan; he and Brenner — who is both his grad school professor and the assistant principal of a charter school in the South Bronx — have bonded over their shared alma mater. Brenner selects four more twentysomethings to role-play as sixth-graders. He calls them to the corner and whispers their assignments out of Eagon's earshot: "Ryan, you're clueless. Jess, you struggle but get there." Colleen and Kathryn are allowed to get things right. They return to the center of the room, and Eagon begins, addressing his mock class:

"We're gonna review some of the information about major religions we've talked about the last few days in preparation for our quiz tomorrow. Stand with one thumb on your chairs and silently push them in. ... What is one of the world's oldest monotheistic religions, Ryan?"

"Mmmm..."

"Can someone help him out? What's one of the world's oldest monotheistic religions, Colleen?"

"One of the world's oldest monotheistic religions is Judaism."

"Ryan, what is it?"

"Ummm..."

"The answer that was just given?"

"One of the world's oldest monotheistic religions is..."

"Colleen, one more time?"

"Judaism."

"Great. Ryan, just the name?"

"Judaism."

"And what does monotheistic mean, Kathryn?"

"Monotheistic means you believe in only one god."

Eagon finishes the oral drill a few minutes later, and the room erupts into applause. Then his classmates — all middle school social studies teachers, most in their first year on the job — do a play-by-play analysis of the performance they'd just cheered. They liked his pacing and varying tone of voice. They dispute whether he should have always insisted on responses in the form of complete sentences. They agree he did well formulating questions and reinforcing the answers for the kid who was struggling.

Welcome to the new Relay Graduate School of Education, a leader in the burgeoning movement to overhaul the way America trains teachers for work in the highest-needs schools. The future of teacher preparation shifts the emphasis from liberal arts-type studies to game day strategies, banking on the successes of real-life teachers running highly managed classrooms. These strategies are exceptionally nuanced and difficult for a new teacher to master, but they produce winning results in educating low-income, minority kids and closing the achievement gap. The orderly learning environment they create is too often a marked contrast to the daily realities of life in violence-ridden urban areas, and it creates the stability that children growing up in such environments need as a prerequisite to thrive. The name "Relay" comes from the idea that a kid with three terrific teachers three years in a row can beat the odds, while a kid with successive lousy teachers is doomed.

Most people agree that traditional education schools have failed, especially in preparing teachers equipped for the realities of high-poverty schools. New York's first independently credentialed graduate school of education in 80 years, Relay is all about getting results in those places. To earn a master's degree, teachers must demonstrate that their students have made a year's growth in a year's time. The dean finds that bar uninspiring, but making high-stakes decisions with only one year of data is risky, so she'd best be prudent.

Gone are courses on education theory and history with no practical bearing on the life of Bryon Eagon, who is in his first year teaching sixth-grade social studies at Kings Collegiate Charter School in Brownsville, one of the poorest neighborhoods in Brooklyn. Gone are courses entirely, actually. Relay has developed more than 60 modules on particular techniques that teachers review together on one Saturday and two weeknights a month. Given their crazy schedules — right now, nearly all are teaching full time at extended-day charter schools — they are allowed to demonstrate proficiency on a lesson in advance and then stay home on the day it's taught. Relay administrators don't care how much time their charges spend sitting in lectures; they care that they know their stuff. Professors aren't lofty academics; they are accomplished practitioners in the field.

Relay has no campus, either, a strategic move to keep tuition low and keep new teachers where the action is — in the schools. Much of the learning takes place in their own classrooms, on Flip cameras, which Relay gives them for both assignments and self-analysis. They don't have to buy many expensive textbooks, but two books that are treated like bibles are Doug Lemov's *Teach Like a Champion* and Paul Bambrick-Santoyo's *Driven by Data: A Practical Guide to Improve Instruction* (see Chapter 4 for a full explanation of Lemov's techniques). Eagon typically tapes himself teaching two or three times a week so he can dissect his own performance. "It's weird, but it's helpful," he said of watching himself.

An outdated model of preparation is one of the great inhibitors for new teachers in all schools, and particularly those serving low-income, minority children. "By almost any standard, many if not most of the nation's 1,450 schools, colleges, and departments of education are doing a mediocre job of preparing teachers for the realities of the 21st-century classroom," U.S. Secretary of Education

Arne Duncan said in the fall of 2009 in a speech at Columbia University's Teachers College. "America's university-based teacher preparation programs need revolutionary change, not evolutionary tinkering." The director of Harvard's Teacher Education Program said during a panel discussion in Washington that year that of the nation's education schools, "100 of them are really worthwhile and the other 1,200 could be shut down tomorrow."

Incubation for Innovation

The idea for Relay was born in 2006 over a dinner between two friends, Norman Atkins and David Levin, who just so happen to be among the best and brightest figures in the charter school world. Atkins is the founder of Uncommon Schools. Levin is the co-founder of the Knowledge Is Power Program, or KIPP. Their charter networks have demonstrated to the nation that closing the achievement gap is totally possible; it just takes a lot of hard work. They talked about how they wanted to grow their networks (Uncommon now has 28 schools, KIPP has 109) and how they would need to fill them with strong teachers. They talked about how their existing teachers often don't learn necessary skills in other preparation programs, and about how they wanted to share best practices from their schools with as broad an audience of teachers as possible. They decided they wanted to start training teachers themselves.

They brought on board Dacia Toll, co-founder of the Achievement First network (20 schools), the third in their trifecta of no-excuses charters, all with high expectations, extra-long instructional days, and extraordinary results. Together they went to Arthur Levine, former president of Columbia's Teachers College, who made waves that year with his report *Educating School Teachers,* in which he famously compared teacher education in the United States to Dodge City, an abject failure. They asked him where to begin. He suggested that they find a partner open to incubating their ideas in an existing education school, since New York requires teachers to have a master's degree or be working toward one, and getting credentialed to award master's degrees is no small feat.

David Steiner, dean of the Hunter College School of Education, was eager to shake things up and waiting with open arms. Together they began developing Teacher U, a practice-based master's program incubated at Hunter. (Steiner would go on to become the New York state education commissioner, but he resigned amid the quagmire of bureaucracy and is now back at Hunter.) With everyone chomping at the bit to get started, Teacher U opened in 2007 perhaps before it was ready, and the first year was a hectic one with high attrition in the pilot class.[1] Things were running more smoothly by year two, but for several reasons the founders wanted to continue the pursuit of becoming their own graduate school. They wanted financial sustainability. They wanted to bypass some of Hunter's required courses. They wanted students to be able to go as fast or as slow as they wanted through the program. "There's just a whole lot of logistical challenges staying in someone else's university," Atkins said. "It's in the DNA of the founders to start from scratch. In some ways, Relay is like a charter school of education. It's significant that we decided to become a higher education institution. We recognize that there's value in reforming higher ed from within higher ed."

The New York State Board of Regents chartered the Relay Graduate School of Education in February 2011 over the protests of several deans of the city's existing education schools, who didn't want added competition during tough economic times. Hunter is part of the City University of New York system, and the CUNY chancellor said the existing Teacher U partnership could accomplish the same goal. (A $30 million grant from the Robin Hood Foundation and investments from other backers including the Bill & Melinda Gates Foundation followed the founders.) The protests also involved Relay's tight focus on classroom techniques, and in recommending approval of the charter, a state-appointed panel cautioned that graduate schools must produce scholarly research.

Teacher U's last class is finishing up this spring, and Relay's inaugural class of 250 New York City teachers began last summer.[2] All were drawn from charter schools, the only places hiring, with many assigned through Teach For America, another Relay partner. The intention is to draw from regular public schools as soon as the city's hiring freeze lifts. Relay officials are eager to work with teachers in environments that aren't as supportive as the no-excuses charters, where sometimes the assignments and feedback Relay provides are redundant.

Relay also started a certificate program last year for 69 teachers in Newark, N.J., that is virtually identical to the master's program in New York. Unlike its neighbor across the Hudson River, New Jersey does not require its teachers to have master's degrees, but Relay would still like to award them and was in the process of applying for a state credential.[3] The vision is to keep expanding so that, in a decade from now, 10,000 teachers in cities around the country are enrolled in an umbrella of Relays.

Giving His All

As an undergraduate at the University of Wisconsin, Bryon Eagon double majored in politics and communications. In 2008, he took a semester off to work as a student organizer for President Barack Obama's election campaign, helping to produce a record turnout of young voters in his home state. Thoroughly bitten by the politics bug, he decided to run for the Madison City Council and was elected an alderman in the spring of 2009. College students had served on the council before, but Eagon was by far the youngest member during the time he was there. He completed his two-year term a few months after his December 2010 college graduation. He was selected for Teach For America during an extraordinarily competitive year, given the economy, and assigned to his top-choice city, New York.

The jury is still out on whether teaching will be a career for Eagon, who is thin and clean-cut with sandy brown hair and thick-rimmed glasses. He could be one of the Teach For America corps members who go on after their two-year commitment expires to public policy careers where they advocate for education reforms. He is thoroughly fascinated by our nation's political system, but education is what's in his blood. His parents both work at the University of Wisconsin–Fox Valley, his mother directing an early childhood center and his father an assistant dean. Two years before Eagon, his older brother did Teach For America in Brooklyn while enrolled at Fordham's Graduate School of Education, and he is now getting a second master's degree in education at Harvard.

For right now, Eagon can't think about the future. He is working too hard.

Each morning he rides from trendy Prospect Heights to Brownsville, a majority black neighborhood dominated by public housing projects. By 6:45 a.m. he arrives at Kings Collegiate,

Bryon Eagon appreciates Relay's practical, hands-on approach to guide him through his first-year teaching.

which is part of the Uncommon Schools network and serves 280 fifth- through eighth-graders in a building shared with another middle school. The instructional day runs until 3:30 p.m. for regular classes, and then there's mandatory enrichment until 4:30. Formal tutoring once a week goes until 5:30. Eagon is often at school until 6:30 p.m. tutoring, preparing lesson plans, or catching up on emails. Then he goes home to start grading papers and doing his Relay assignments. His Crunch gym membership lies dormant. All he can think about on the weekends when he's not working is catching up on sleep (and maybe watching a little football). He is giving his all, yet he worries about whether it's enough. "I hope I've been contributing as much as I've been learning," he said.

Eagon hears from his brother that Relay is prompting discussion among graduate students at Harvard about what the role of a school of education should be. (The Ivy League in general and Harvard in particular are very well-represented among Relay's leadership.) Eagon is personally quite pleased with Relay, which this year is charging $4,500 in tuition; prices for future students will go up somewhat once they can apply for financial aid.[4] The strategies Eagon is learning have been highly relevant, particularly as he works to get a handle on classroom management. "When I'm looking at my students' data, I'm less concerned about the philosophy of education or the history of American schools than I am about what I'm going to do differently," Eagon said, referring to what is typically taught in education graduate schools. "As a first-year teacher, this is what matters to me now. I wrote a few papers on John Dewey back in college. History and philosophy are both interesting and important, but in the limited time we have as teachers, what I need are the hands-on practices to get my teaching up."

By early December, Eagon had already been observed twice by Relay's dean, once by a Teach For America representative with a second visit scheduled, and at least three times by Uncommon administrators. He estimates that a Kings Collegiate staff member is in his room three times a week, and he gets ongoing coaching from the school's dean of curriculum. "It's a little overwhelming at times, but I'd rather be overwhelmed with oversupport than undersupported," he said. He has been working on getting to know the fifth-graders while on cafeteria and boys bathroom duty and in a small guided reading session he leads for a half-dozen kids every afternoon. He's heard that building relationships with them this year will pay off with classroom management next year.

Eagon put meticulous attention into decorating his classroom. A blowup globe hangs from the center of the ceiling. Every inch of wall space is filled with something: photos of a smiling Eagon and students, examples of excellent student work, posters on China to India to Egypt. Flags from Haiti, Barbados, Jamaica, Guyana, and, naturally, Wisconsin fly. In the center of the front wall Eagon has posted his big, bigger, and biggest goals for his three daily social studies classes, which are tracked by reading ability. Big goal: "Every student will achieve at least 80% mastery on homework, class work, and quizzes." Bigger goal: "Every student will think, speak, write, and act like a historian." Biggest goal: "EVERY student will go to college (and the lucky ones will attend the University of Wisconsin)." On the shelf are admissions materials from Eagon's alma mater. With so much to look at, students don't usually notice the tripod above the sink in the back left corner. They don't realize that a camera atop that tripod is often running, and their teacher is tracking his every move.

From Theory to Practice

Research has shown that a teacher having a master's degree in education does not necessarily translate into higher student achievement. Debates rage about how to fix these broken graduate programs, but most can agree that practicality is the critical element generally lacking. Theory and practice are often pitted against each other as an either-or scenario. Relay Provost Brent Maddin said the key isn't to weed out theory but rather to distill it down to essential points for an extremely busy teacher. "As a profession, we're horrible at translating theory to practice," he said. In response to years of criticism, several historically theory-based programs are adding practice components. Arizona State University, home to the nation's largest teacher preparation program, this academic year began requiring undergraduate education majors to do a yearlong apprenticeship working with a mentor teacher. New York has been a breeding ground for innovative new techniques. In addition to licensing Relay, the state awarded $12.5 million in grants for promising programs, including an urban residency program for science teachers at the American Museum of Natural History. The state is moving in the direction of Relay by phasing in a system where all teachers will need to demonstrate their students' achievement to be awarded a master's degree in education.

At a recent Wednesday night data-analysis session with teachers in a basement school auditorium in Bedford-Stuyvesant, Relay Dean Mayme Hostetter begins with a clip from the 2004 movie *Man on Fire*. Denzel Washington's character needs to figure out why the girl he is coaching in swimming struggles at meets but not during practice. It turns out she's scared of the starting pistol. The video is a "hook," a technique from *Teach Like a Champion* to engage children at the beginning of a class, but the strategy works for adults as well. Hostetter's point is that they need to comb the data to figure out specifically where their students are getting stuck.

Hostetter and Maddin have the daunting yet enviable job of figuring out how to create great teachers out of everyone enrolled at Relay. They have spent so many hours together on this question that last summer she was the "best Mayme" in his wedding. They have cubicles in a sixth-floor office in the Flatiron district, where Relay's staff of 50 is based, but often they are out in the field. They toured 60 high-performing urban schools when they first came to Relay in 2008. Based on what they saw and their own experiences as successful teachers, they developed five guiding principles for their program. One: The teacher creates a strong classroom culture where kids feel empowered and connected to each other. Two: The teacher has a deep understanding of who she is and who the students are. Three: The teacher meticulously plans lessons at the unit and yearlong levels. Four: The teacher's content knowledge is deep and flexible ("you not only know how to add fractions fluently yourself in five different ways, but you know how to teach kids to do it," Hostetter said). Five: The teacher pays attention to details in setting academic goals and tracking progress. "I wouldn't go so far as to say there's a recipe, but you see far more similarities than differences among these 60 schools, and that fuels our collective belief that teachers are built and not born," said Maddin, a National Board Certified teacher who helped found a charter school in Texas. "If we thoughtfully construct a curriculum that teachers take over two years, it should lead to increased student achievement in their classrooms, which helps me wake up in the morning."

To take the curriculum further, they'd like to leverage online resources to help teachers get more training in how to teach their specific subjects. A biology teacher doesn't necessarily need a bunch of advanced science courses but does need to dive into how to best teach biology. They're also interested in character development, holding teachers accountable for helping their students develop as people. And they'd like to build on the training they offer in building relationships across racial and class lines. "It's huge and it's one of the biggest struggles for new teachers in classrooms different than what they grew up in," said Hostetter, who used to teach in the South Bronx. "It's a hard thing for people to talk about and an even harder thing to teach about."

An inherently imperfect and ever-evolving process is how to evaluate teachers based on student achievement. Most of those enrolled at Relay are elementary school teachers, and in their classes Relay can track reading growth to determine whether a child has made a year's progress. For Eagon and other teachers of specific content, the bar for Relay graduation is whether their students can master at least 70 percent of the material. Standardized test scores are used to determine whether someone graduates from Relay with distinction but not whether they graduate at all. Teachers analyze their students' performance during the first year and are held accountable for results in the second.

If Hostetter and Maddin could wave a magic wand, they would like to figure out a way for first-year teachers not to have to work full time. They see many like Bryon Eagon. "They're working really, really, really hard," Hostetter said. On the Saturday Eagon did the oral drill in Brenner's class, administrators were visiting from MATCH Corps, a highly competitive yearlong fellowship program in Boston that trains new teachers while having them work part time as charter school tutors. The model intrigues Hostetter. On the flip side, she said, those working full time while at Relay "really do feel a sense of ownership and urgency around their students and their students' learning. They are hungry to do right by their kids."

Game Time

Eagon is about to deliver another oral drill. This time he is in dress clothes. The camera is on, and the sixth-graders are actual children. The topic is geography of ancient India. Objective: Students will be able to identify major geographic features.

"When I say so," he begins to the 24 students in royal blue monogrammed shirts over navy sweaters and navy pants, "you are going to rise and push in your chairs and stand behind them. Today is out of eight points. ... We're waiting for silence. There are six questions but eight points. You can easily earn one point — I call it a free point — for standing up silently and pushing in your chairs. Shhh. So far we're not on track for that free point. There's also a free point when we're done when you sit down silently. ... If you need to remind yourself to not turn around, you can put your hands on your chair. When I read the question" — he pauses for talking to stop — "When I read the question, do not raise your hand even if you're really excited and you know you know the answer. We've done it before; let's do it right again. Let's start by getting that first easy point by everyone silently standing up and pushing in your chairs. We're going to be there in five ... four ... three ... give me your voices off, two ... one. Hands down on your chair. Thank you. That was one free point. First question, again, please do not raise your hands. Number one, Isaiah facing forward, what continent is India located on, Octavia?[5] What continent is India located on?"

"Asia."

"Asia is correct. That's a point." To the class: "You can also lose a point if there's talking between questions. Number two, what is one of the two major rivers in India, what is one of the two major rivers in India, Cassandra?"

"The Indus River."

"The Indus River is one. That is a point. Number three, what's another major river, Sharif?"

"The Ganges."

"The Ganges, correct. That's another point. Again, you're facing forward, hands on your chair please, Stephon, standing up straight. Number four, what is the whole mountain range in the northeast corner of India, Mya?"

"The Himalayas."

"The Himalayas is correct. Number five, what is the terminology that describes why India is isolated because it's surrounded by three bodies of water and the Himalayan Mountains, Shawn? Since there's talking we're just going to move on to the next question without this answer. Number six, what is the name of the strong winds that blow one direction in the winter and another direction in the summer that bring in the rainfall, Jody?"

She hesitates. Eagon repeats: "The strong winds."

"Monsoon?"

"A monsoon is correct. Now let's get another free point by silently taking a seat and opening up your packet to page 2 ..."

Seven out of eight points. Not bad, but reviewing the "game film" later, Eagon isn't satisfied. He needs to improve on giving explicit directions and making sure students follow them. He's seen videos at Relay of exemplar oral drills, so he can compare his video and target specific areas for growth. "I need to keep tweaking my directions, expectations, and compliance," he said, "until I get it just right."

Endnotes

1. The Teacher U pilot class consisted primarily of experienced teachers from other states in need of a New York credential; it ended up merging with Teacher U's second class, eligible for a master's degree in 2010. Most of the original group of 30 did not complete the program. Relay now serves predominantly first- and second-year teachers.

2. Teacher U awarded 103 master's degrees in 2010 and 112 in 2011. Its last class enrolled 150 students.

3. Relay's application to award master's degrees in New Jersey was still pending at press time.

4. Relay was in the midst of a process to enable students in the New York program to apply for financial aid. However, the school is committed to staying affordable for new teachers.

5. Student names have been changed.

In Colorado Springs, superintendent Mike Miles designed what is regarded as the nation's most innovative teacher pay system.

Chapter 6

BOOSTING TEACHER QUALITY

Recent research into the question of how much teacher effectiveness matters — a little, a fair amount, a lot — has produced strikingly clear results. To draw on a cliché, teacher quality is pretty much the whole ball of wax. The good news is that researchers, educators, and even union leaders now agree that improving teacher quality should be the top priority. The less encouraging news lies in the uncomfortable reality that school districts have spent at least the last two decades hiring, promoting, and granting tenure to teachers who weren't always the best and brightest. Probably even longer than two decades.

Why did that happen? And, more importantly, how do we get ourselves out of this mess?

The "why" is no mystery. For decades, schools were able to effortlessly draw the brightest females and minorities into teaching because the private sector, for the most part, shunned them. MaryEllen Elia, 63, the superintendent of schools in Tampa profiled in Chapter 3, recalls that when she graduated from college, most females assumed they had two career choices: nursing or teaching. "A whole lot of graduates didn't have many options, so they went into teaching. Now, corporations are searching for ways to get women and minorities into positions. They'll pay more and value them more." The effect on African American male teachers is especially striking: Today, fewer than 1 in 50 teachers is a black male. That private-sector shunning of women and minorities ended long ago, but from the perspective of the school districts, it might as well have been overnight. Oddly, school district human relations departments seem to have barely noticed these dramatic changes and, for the most part, just keep accepting candidates from the same pipelines.

Now the what-do-we-do-about-it question.

Many governors, mayors, and education reformers have concluded that the solution lies in making teaching more attractive by making it more respected, which starts with tying compensation to effectiveness. Instead of paying teachers for their longevity (when all research points to the fact that a six-year veteran may very well be a better teacher than a 26-year veteran), reward them for boosting student learning. "Because you breathe you shouldn't automatically get a salary increase," Elia said. "Salary increases should be based on things that relate to children." And, of nearly automatically granting teachers tenure after two years of lightly scrutinized teaching, make tenure something that is earned by demonstrating quality. A hallmark of all respected professions is a high threshold for entering.

All this starts with ushering in real teacher evaluations, something that school districts have never done. If school leaders can't identify good teaching, they have no way of improving struggling teachers, paying the best teachers more, or getting rid of those who will never improve student learning. There's real progress to be reported with teacher evaluations: Over the past three years, nearly two-thirds of the states have made serious changes to their teacher evaluation systems. As of 2012, annual teacher evaluations were required in 25 states, with nearly that many states requiring that evaluations include some proof of student learning growth — a development that not long ago was considered unimaginable.

True, teacher evaluations are a work in progress, but school chiefs almost universally agree that shifting to a system that rewards teaching competence is the future. Said Kaya Henderson, schools chancellor in Washington, D.C.: "A great teacher is not going to teach harder or better because there's a bonus. But if they make a significant accomplishment, treating them the same way we treat the teacher who sent their kids backward makes no sense ... This whole one-size-fits-all approach is so counter to me. There are very few occupations that have a lockstep pay schedule ... I'm in a situation where right now I have to change outcomes for kids. I don't have the money to raise teachers' salaries to $100,000 across the board. But I do have the money to reward my highest-performing teachers."[1]

The leaders in the pay-scale reform movement, including the districts in Houston, Tampa, and Washington, draw close scrutiny from other school districts considering the same. The same holds true for states pushing the envelope, such as Colorado, Rhode Island, and Tennessee. What seems to draw little attention nationally, however, is that one school district, Harrison School District Two in Colorado Springs, has not only successfully completed the reforms that other districts are just starting, but it accomplished the dramatic changes with surprisingly little rancor. Today, Harrison has settled into a private-sector style pay-for-performance system that other school districts only dream about.

Can other school districts successfully imitate Harrison? A visit to Colorado Springs leads to some unexpected observations about that possibility.

The Mike Miles Story

Given superintendents' longstanding acceptance of personnel systems that rarely evaluate teachers and compensate them with lockstep pay schedules that ignore actual job performance, it should not come as a surprise that the first superintendent to turn that upside down comes from outside the profession. That's the case with Mike Miles, who grew up in a military family, graduated from West Point, became an Army Ranger and company commander, left to earn graduate degrees from the University of California at Berkeley in Slavic languages and Columbia University in international affairs, joined the foreign service, served tours as a diplomat in Poland and Russia, and then, at the age of 39, decided upon his true calling: teaching.

Miles, 55, one of eight children of an African American father and Japanese mother, always had an interest in education, the result of being rescued by two first-grade teachers in Colorado Springs who helped him overcome a speech problem that had him unable to pronounce many words. "At the time, my father was stationed in Korea, and it was tough for my mother, who had these eight kids running around and didn't speak English well herself," he said. "The teachers stepped in to help, and for a year and a half, they used a tape recorder to teach me how to speak." Miles, who is very aware of the fates of many black boys with learning disabilities, realizes how close he came to being another depressing statistic. Instead, he went on to be his high school valedictorian, then was off to West Point. "I am eternally grateful to those teachers," he said. "Eternally grateful."

Upon leaving the Foreign Service, Miles discovered a program at the University of Colorado, Colorado Springs for earning alternative teaching certifications. After six months there, he took a job as a high school teacher. After four years of teaching, he was appointed principal of a middle school. After four years as principal, he was promoted to assistant superintendent. And after three years on that job, he saw the superintendent's position open up at a neighboring school district, Harrison School District Two, which had long been the lowest-performing (and highest-poverty) district in Colorado Springs (40 percent Latino, 21 percent African American, with nearly 80 percent of the 10,500 students qualifying for free or reduced-price lunches).[2] "I wanted to go to a school district that had an at-risk population," Miles said.

Miles won the Harrison superintendent's job for the 2006-07 school year. Before officially taking over, he spent two months visiting classrooms. He was not encouraged by what he saw. "The instruction was terrible," he said. "It was instruction by worksheet. What standards they had appeared to be almost irrelevant. There was very little directed instruction, very little engagement. We had teachers who hadn't been evaluated in six years. Administrators were not walking through the classrooms; nobody knew what was going on in the classrooms." It quickly became clear to Miles that poverty alone couldn't explain why Harrison schools were nearly at the bottom of the list that ranked Colorado schools by performance. "Harrison was doing poorly because it was not working effectively as a school district," Miles said. "No question. There was no sense of urgency. No focus on instruction. We had an organization designed to reinforce the status quo."

The newly elected school board that chose Miles was reform-oriented and expected big changes from him. He delivered. Miles discovered that previous superintendents had hewn to a tradition of following the policy decisions made by a 21-person committee that included 14 union officials and required a near-unanimous vote (20 out of 21) to approve change. "I got to the first meeting and a union teacher came up to me [and] said I could do nothing unless this committee agreed," Miles said. "Even a Boy Scout troop of 12-year-olds could not have a stupider rule. This was an example of a school system purposefully designed to avoid change." So he disbanded the existing panel and drew up a new panel with new rules — rules that needed the approval of the superintendent and board.

Next came the discovery that teachers were allowed to take "docked days," where any teacher could simply not show up for work as long as he or she agreed to not take pay for that day. More than 100 teachers had each taken more than 20 docked days. Miles ended that practice. Another shock arose when Miles issued a simple edict: Keep your classroom doors open and expect observers. "Based on the reaction, with newspaper editorials and angry people, you would have thought I shot someone," he recalled. "Their attitude: How dare you make a unilateral decision? But you walk around today, and you'll see that all the classroom doors are open and nobody minds. It was the most important instructional decision I made, and it didn't cost any more, didn't take any training. But it had to be done. How do you build a professional organization that's a learning community when you lock the doors and put construction paper over the windows?"

All that time, Miles was quietly preparing for his far bigger reform: a teacher compensation system based on competency rather than number of years in the classroom. The problem with traditional teacher compensation systems, argues Miles, is that the pay system is disconnected from the central goal of the organization to improve student learning. "Salaries are the biggest part of any school district budget, as much as 80 percent, and yet those salaries are disconnected from what we value," he said. "I don't think any organization is going to maximize effectiveness if they have that big a disconnect between what they value and how they compensate people."

By the 2008-09 school year, Miles was ready to move. New teacher evaluations were in place, and his concept paper on restructuring salaries to match the results of the compensation won board approval. By the next year, teachers were placed on an effectiveness scale based on their evaluations, where student test results made up half the score. Multiple measures of student achievement were based either on academic growth or comparing students' scores to those of their academic peers. The following year, 2010-11, Harrison School District Two entered a zone no other school district has experienced: salaries — not just bonuses — based on demonstrated competency. That put Harrison four years ahead of the Colorado law that requires all school districts to usher in evaluations with consequences.

Harrison now distributes salary money under a nine-level compensation system, with one exception: During the transition period, veteran teachers — regardless of their ratings — are protected against salary cuts. Instead, veteran teachers with poor ratings get flatlined while younger teachers with high ratings get salary hikes. For example, Harrison now has some highly rated third-year teachers making $54,000 a year (a good salary in that region). Under the old lockstep salary schedule, it would have taken those teachers between 12 and 13 years to reach that level of compensation.

What's striking about Harrison is the acceptance of the system. Observers of school districts with rough-edged labor relations would have (accurately) predicted a teacher revolt. Instead, nearly 80 percent of the Harrison teachers, based on district surveys, agree with their placements. Even more surprising about the Harrison pay plan is the near absence of teacher firings. Miles estimates that when he arrived, about a third of the teachers were effective, another third were capable of reaching that level, and the bottom third had very little chance. Yes, teachers were fired based on the new evaluation system. But for the most part, the low-rated teachers — along with better teachers who didn't like the new evaluation system — simply left. It's a natural sorting system, resulting in few firings, that allows Miles to shift to a system where nearly all teachers are effective.

Teachers Take Notice

No teacher takes a job in Harrison without knowing that something radical awaits them. All applicants get handed a tersely written two-page memo titled "Looking for Heroes." Samples from that memo (words in bold as they appear):

*— We need to inform you that it is **harder to work in the Harrison District than almost any other district in Colorado.***

— You will be continuously coached and will be subject to numerous spot observations. You will teach with the door open.

— We will monitor your progress and evaluate you fairly, but accurately. The expectations are high as is the **accountability** *for improving instruction. And* **the search for excellence will be relentless.**

— **If you are given to excuse-making or blaming our parents or students, do not come to the Harrison School District.** *If you fear accountability, do not have a commitment to excellence, or have a need to fight for adult issues over the issues of students, do not come to the Harrison District. You will be gravely disappointed, as will we.*

Sounds daunting. The impact on recruiting teachers, however, is minimal, principals report. For one thing, within a few years all school districts in Colorado will have similar systems. Therefore, teachers wishing to avoid serious evaluations will have to leave the state. Plus, many new teachers eager to prove their merits are drawn to private-sector-style accountability. "Honestly, a lot of teachers just gravitate to this district because of that," said Cheri Martinez, principal of Harrison High School. "They are hungry for this because they don't want to be in a system that's stagnant and just checks the boxes. They want to get paid for doing a good job."

But the bigger reason for the near-absence of strife over the changes here is the "sorting" issue: Teachers who don't like it end up leaving, one way or another. "I had a kindergarten teacher who came to our school from another state who felt sorry for kids living in poverty," said Wendy Birhanzel, principal of Centennial Elementary School, the highest-poverty elementary school in the district. "She would talk about the mom who isn't there at night and dad working two jobs." Those children, the teacher argued, should not be required to meet the school goal stipulating that all children be able to write a paragraph by the end of the school year. Birhanzel told her that "we don't care to let poverty be an excuse. We care about what you're doing in the instructional day, and we expect all children to be able to write a paragraph." That teacher was gone by the end of the year.

The Collaboration Question

Nationally, the objection to moving to a Harrison-style system is that competitive pay will fracture the all-important staff collaboration needed for teamwork-style teaching. "The fear with teacher evaluations tied to student achievement is that they would trigger more competition, and teachers would hoard their lessons and see their colleagues more as competitors," Miles said. "That has not turned out to be the case." Teachers figured out they had to collaborate to succeed. And collaboration, including mentoring other teachers, is built into the evaluation system. At Harrison, no teacher can earn the top "distinguished" rating without demonstrating leadership within the school. "Anyone who is distinguished," Miles said, "can't be a lone ranger."

Interviews with principals bore that out. They said collaboration has only intensified. At Harrison High School, some veteran teachers take notice when younger teachers draw higher ratings, Martinez said. "They think, 'I need to go see those teachers to gain instructional strategies.' It's not just about the money that's driving them. It's looking around and saying, 'Hey, this person is achieving. What can I do?' You know things are changing for the better when you have veterans going to watch second- or even first-year teachers." Teachers earn leadership points by coaching other teachers. "They have to help other teachers," Martinez said, "so you can't just shut your door. They have to share to get their leadership points. If you're not getting those points you won't move up. It won't happen."

How It Looks in the Classroom

It is midmorning at Soaring Eagles Elementary, and Principal Kelli O'Neil prowls the hallways looking for classrooms to observe. O'Neil oversees a school where students score far higher than what might be predicted based on the school's 50 percent poverty level. These classroom observations are integral to that success, and O'Neil knows exactly what she is looking for. Are the objectives on the board? Are all the kids engaged? Is the teacher getting multiple responses to the teacher's queries? Is the teacher's lesson aligned with the district objectives? Is it in sync with the district's academic calendar?

At her first stop, a kindergarten class not far from her office, O'Neil is pleased by what she sees from a third-year teacher. "This teacher is working on alliteration, and she has great engagement in her classroom," O'Neil says. "As you can see, she's getting multiple responses and the kids are really comfortable." O'Neil has picked this teacher to groom for leadership despite her relative inexperience. "She just has a classroom awareness that some teachers don't have," she said.

The next visit is to a classroom run by a veteran teacher with whom more proficient students had been placed. To an outsider, everything in the classroom appears calm and orderly, with students either working in a group with the teacher, going over a book they are reading, or working independently on assigned projects. But O'Neil is not happy with what she sees. "I see very little rigor here," she says. Even the quiet bothers her: "In the previous classroom, you saw the energy level. The teacher was very dynamic. In this class, it feels like the air was sucked out of the room."

O'Neil frowns as she studies the wall where teachers are required to post daily objectives. "You can see that she doesn't have the objective tied to the content of what's being taught," she says. More frowns come from O'Neil as she observes how the teacher keeps the students on task — with a glare directed at the offending student. "Instead of reguiding the student to what they should be doing, she gives them a dirty look. So her student interactions are not positive. Students who are not happy in their environment are not going to learn at the same rate as kids who are excited."

Based on test scores alone, this teacher's class might look good, but she's teaching students who started at a higher proficiency level. "She doesn't have enough students reading at the advanced level," O'Neil said. "I've seen more advanced readers in some of our general education classes." And that will be caught in the teacher's evaluations, when her students are compared with similarly proficient students at other Harrison schools. Also affecting this teacher's performance ratings will be the critical comments coming from multiple classroom visits made by O'Neil and her staff. Although the staff at Soaring Eagles is working with the teacher to improve her instruction, O'Neil is not sure about the outcome. The teacher is resisting the outside guidance, O'Neil said, and is disinterested in trying to move to a higher rating. Again, the sorting at work.

O'Neil's next stop is at the classroom of art teacher Bobbi Jackson. When Miles first began planning his pay-for-performance system he considered omitting difficult-to-evaluate positions such as gym and art teachers. That didn't last past the first meeting with teachers. The gym and art teachers were adamant: Include us! For art teachers, the system is "challenging," Jackson concedes, but worth it. "It shows people that what we do is valued and it shows people that we are actually teaching the kids and that they are actually learning," she said.

Are Harrison Reforms Working? Are They Replicable?

As of the 2011-12 school year, Harrison was only in its second year of a pay-for-performance system. Answering the question of whether to pay teachers for how well they boost student performance will take several more years. For Miles, that target year is 2016, when he expects Harrison students to perform at the state average and the graduation rate to reach 90 percent.[3] "That may not sound like much of a goal," Miles said, "but the state average for poverty is 38 percent. We're at 77 percent, and a lot of the kids who come to us are way behind in their reading, writing, and math. So reaching the state average would be pretty incredible for us." The early signs are promising, with Harrison students' scores rising faster than the state average. "Already we're well above the competition," Miles said, referring to other districts in the state with a high concentration of poor minority students.

Also encouraging is the fiscal stability of the pay-for-performance system. When the system launched, 47 percent of the district budget went toward teachers' salaries. "We designed the program so that it will never go above 52 percent," Miles said. The fact that the Harrison system is all-encompassing — not just a bonus system — is an important point. School districts that rely on handing out bonuses to exemplary teachers, bonuses that in some cases come from foundations, eventually have to find the extra bonus money on their own. This program is designed to be sustainable.

Other savings going toward boosting teacher salaries include doing away with paying more for extra graduate degrees (a staple of all school districts that researchers have never been able to connect to improved student learning) and bonuses for mentoring newer teachers. To achieve the very top rating in Harrison, mentoring is simply expected — and part of the evaluation criteria. "When I first arrived in Poland as a diplomat, nobody got paid to take the new kid under their wing," Miles said. "The other professionals didn't want the new kid to screw things up so they made sure I learned the protocols right away. That's a professional organization; that's what professionals do."

Given the "sorting" that has taken place here, with teachers uncomfortable with the new system or not happy about their ratings likely to leave, an increased turnover rate might be expected. But the pay-for-performance pushed up the turnover rate only slightly. It's unclear how much the recession kept the turnover rate low.

So are other school districts likely to make the same smooth transition to a pay-for-performance system? Here's where the Harrison story gets interesting. This appears to be a school district happy with its reforms, but there is caution about other school districts copying what has happened here. Kelli O'Neil, the Soaring Eagles principal, likens what Miles has done to rebuilding an entire car: "He had this vision, starting five years ago. He didn't just dump it into our laps. We had four years to train, four years to get the right people into the classrooms, four years to learn how to be instructional leaders. We did all that before [the new pay system] came to fruition."

The complexity of the Harrison system is daunting. Different teachers have different "templates" to follow that describe what is expected of them. A regular high school history teacher, for example, has a different template than an AP history teacher. Gym and art teachers require their own templates. In all, the district has 22 templates for elementary school teachers, 20 for middle school teachers, and 46 for high school teachers. "Some of these districts are trying to implement the pay reforms without all that work," O'Neil warned. "I can't even imagine the struggle they are going to go through. Mike is the guy who rebuilt the car. He has a really long-term vision that only his military mind can have. I don't think he sleeps ... and now a lot of districts are going to merely repaint the car and put it into the showroom."

Miles also has doubts about how many districts can replicate what Harrison has done, but his doubts are less about the technical aspects of building a pay-for-performance system. "The tough part is the paradigm shift, a shift in how you get paid and when you get advanced," he said. "How does it feel not to get advanced every year if someone else is getting advanced? Teachers have to get used to the fact that 35 percent of the staff may be getting pretty good raises while 65 percent get no raise. How does that feel? What we're used to in education is, everybody gets 3 percent raises. If one person gets a step raise just for living another year, everybody gets it."

It's not clear how many school districts will attempt to merely repaint the car. Nor is it clear how many districts are willing to embrace a paradigm shift that would discard not just the lockstep pay system but also the extra pay for graduate degrees and mentoring other teachers. What is clear from visiting Colorado Springs, however, is that what may be the single most urgent reform needed in public education is doable — and achievable with tolerable angst.

How the Mike Miles system fares in a larger district is about to get a test. In April 2012, Miles was appointed superintendent of the Dallas Independent School District.

Endnotes

1. Lindsey Layton, "As Teacher Merit Pay Spreads, One Noted Voice Cries, 'It Doesn't Work,'" *The Washington Post*, February 15, 2012.

2. Colorado Springs is served by roughly 10 school districts, which is unusual for a city of its size.

3. In 2006, when Miles arrived, the graduation rate was 61 percent. By 2011, that rate reached 72 percent, almost matching the state average.

Part 3

REACHING PARENTS AND PRESCHOOLERS

Emily Thomas gets writing guidance from Jessica Lane, one of three teachers in her preschool classroom, all of whom hold college degrees.

Chapter 7

THE PRESCHOOL POTENTIAL

On this Monday morning, 4-year-old Emily Thomas is pretty in pink, with pink striped leggings and a jacket with pink hearts. Halloween is fast approaching, and Emily thumbs through a Halloween magazine to show a visitor her costume — a princess. "Just like the one in the picture?" Emily smiles, "Um, yeah." Even at age 4, it is easy to predict that Emily will emerge as a striking young woman, an interesting mix of a Korean mother and African American father, a combination that gives her distinctively fluffy black hair.

It is 7:30 a.m., but Emily has been awake since 6 a.m., the usual wakeup time on preschool days. Already, she has consumed her oatmeal with raisins plus a cheese chew stick. Emily is allowed to watch a kids movie while her mother, Kate Heffernan, makes her lunch. Emily and her mother share the only bedroom in a tiny apartment stuffed with toys. Soon, Heffernan will drive Emily to an AppleTree Early Learning Public Charter School a few miles from their apartment, where Emily will stay from 8 a.m. to 5 p.m., when Heffernan will pick her up after working her shift at the Gap. Emily's father ("We plan to get married") lives in Virginia, where he works as a warehouseman at the Pentagon.

When Emily was 18 months old, it became clear she was having some speech delay problems. She just wasn't babbling like the other toddlers. As she grew older, she had trouble answering questions, especially about her emotions. Happy? Sad? Heffernan is sensitive to speech delay issues. Born in Korea, she was adopted by an American family and brought to the United States at age 2½. The dramatic switch in languages at such a young age left her with verbal issues to overcome.

American Preschool History

Emily may come from a low-income family, and she may have some mild learning challenges to overcome, but in landing a spot at AppleTree, she has essentially won the school lottery. In fact, AppleTree may have the potential to achieve the kind of results turned in by the nation's legendary preschool experiment, the Perry Preschool in Ypsilanti, Mich., a school where from 1962 to 1967 low-income, African American preschoolers ages 3 and 4 were lavished with expert attention. Those students were then matched against an apples-to-apples control group that had no preschool. A research team followed those students through their lives, and the results were remarkable. At age 40, those who experienced the preschool earned more money, were more likely to be employed, had committed fewer crimes, and were more likely to have graduated from high school. The savings, a mix of taxes paid and prison stays avoided, were stunning — as much as $16 in savings per every dollar spent on preschool.

Over the years, cities and states, and most notably the federal government with its massive Head Start program, have tried to reach for similar gains from preschool, and usually come up short. Head Start, for example, never approached Perry in quality, and the gains from Head Start have been modest. In recent years, however, the quality of many programs (Oklahoma, for example, handles its preschool program for 4-year-olds as it would any other grade) has been rising.

Still, few preschools are as well designed and funded as AppleTree, which raises the expectations of Perry-like payoffs for its students. Through several funding sources — $11,500 per student from Washington, another $3,000 per student from Washington for facilities support, another $3,500 per student in state and federal grants — AppleTree is able to spend $18,000 per student, roughly what many elite private schools cost. The money, however, is secondary to the research that goes into a day at AppleTree, with special attention given to developing early literacy skills without ever forcing the young children to endure academic-driven regimes such as flashcards. The education program developed here, called Every Child Ready, is all about turning play into learning opportunities that pay off in later grades.

How It Looks on the Ground

Here's a taste of Emily's day:

....

8–8:45 a.m. — Breakfast is served

Roughly half the class of 20 children shows up for breakfast, on this day an apple, bagel, and a carton of fat-free milk. Teachers on duty include lead teacher Cha Quan Wilder, a graduate of George Mason University with a major in administration of justice, who got into teaching via a teaching fellow position at AppleTree and is currently working on her master's degree at George Mason in educating second language learners; Jessica Lane, a graduate of Miami University of Ohio who majored in English and French and taught abroad in France before launching an education career in the United States, and whose near-term goal is earning a master's in early education; and teaching fellow Rachel Hickman, who earned a bachelor's degree in anthropology from Franklin and Marshall College.

8:45 a.m. — Morning meeting

Each child has an assigned spot on the rug, designed to provide just enough room to avoid bumping into the child "next door," thus avoiding a squirming match. This "advanced organizer," as AppleTree calls it, provides the children with a preview of upcoming events for the day, weaving previously learned material with new material. Before the start of class, Hickman brings each student up to a whiteboard and asks them to vote on their favorite recently assigned book, all clustered around "construction" themes. Did they like *The House that Jack Built*, *Building a House*, or *The Little House*? Each vote is recorded, thus creating graph material for future use.

9:05 a.m. — Preschoolers check themselves into "stations"

Every day, students rotate from station to station, with most of the station work focused on the current theme of building. The usual stations: Library, Writing, Art Easel, Art Studio, Investigation, Location, Construction Zone, Exploration, and Dramatic Play. Students check themselves in and out by moving their detachable nametags from station to station. Emily's first stop is Exploration, where she dons a blue plastic apron and begins moving toy bulldozers and trucks through a box filled with fake dirt. A sign above the box lists the associated vocabulary words: asphalt, build, plan, road, smooth, car, truck, gutter, and sidewalk. Next she moves to the Art Easel, where she paints. The teachers circulate the room carrying out their "facilitation" duties, choosing different students for verbal interactions that follow this pattern:

Teacher: "Tell me about what you're drawing."

Student: "I'm drawing a man moving dirt on his truck" (pointing to a picture from one of the storybooks).

Teacher: "Oh, I see! You're drawing the construction man shoveling dirt on his bulldozer" (truck). "Can you say 'shoveling'?"

Student: "Shoveling."

Teacher: "That's right, the construction man is shoveling, or moving, the dirt with his bulldozer. Let's write down what you just told me. Construction ..." (teacher writes word on top of paper) "man. ... Hmm, I bet you could help me spell this word. Let's sound it out! Mmmm. What letter makes the /m/ sound?"

Student: "M!"

Teacher: "That's right, the letter M makes the /m/ sound. I'll put that here" (writes lowercase "m" to start the word "man" beside "construction"). "The next letter we need to write our word, 'man,' is the /a/ sound. Mmmmm, aaaaan. Mmmmm, aaaaan. What letter makes the /a/ sound?

Student: "E!"

Teacher: "That's a very good guess! The /a/ sound for the letter A and the /e/ sound for the letter E can be very tricky! The letter A makes the /a/ sound, so the next letter we need is A. I'll write that here beside the M" (teacher writes "a" and sounds out /m/ /a/ while writing).

"We have one more letter we need to finish our word, 'man.' Mmmmm, aaaaaaa, nnnnnnn. /N/. What letter makes the /n/ sound?"

Student: "N!"

Teacher: "You are really listening carefully! That's right, the letter N makes the /n/ sound! That's the last letter in our word, 'man.' I'm writing the letter N right here beside M, A, to make the word 'man.' Say 'man.'

Student: "Man."

Teacher: "Yes, m-a-n spells 'man,' and you helped me write it by listening carefully and trying your best. Let's finish writing your sentence. We already have 'construction man,' now I need to add 'shoveling'" (writes shoveling) "'dirt.' /D/, /d/, /d/. What's the first letter I need to write the word 'dirt'?"

Student: "D!"

Teacher: "That's right! D-i-r-t spells 'dirt'" (while writing last word on the paper). "We wrote all your words. Can you read them for me?"

Student : "Construction man shoveling dirt."

Teacher: "You've got it! You remembered our new word, 'shoveling,' and you worked really hard to help me sound out 'man' and 'dirt.' Great work, Jami!"

Student: "Thank you!"

Teacher: "Thank you for telling me about your drawing. I'm going to go help another friend now. Don't forget to put your name on your work so we'll remember it's yours!"

What AppleTree does is turn the corner from the rhyming and alliteration exercises common to all preschools. It's a subtle turn that most observers would never even notice. "We look at different parts of the word," said Lydia Carlis, director of education for AppleTree, who has a doctorate in special education. "Take the word 'bat.' If you remove part of the word, 'bat' without the B, can they say 'at'? Can they take the word 'at' and put the B in front and say 'bat'? It sounds clinical but you can make this into games and songs and fun activities."

The reason they need those skills is that kindergarteners today are being asked to absorb far more advanced literacy skills. Today's kindergartners are expected to handle reading and writing demands that two decades ago were considered second-grade material. "When the children arrive in kindergarten," said Carlis, "there's a huge difference between the children who learned 'bat' from rhyming and alliteration and those who learned how to break and rebuild the sounds. They don't need to be reading by the time they get to kindergarten, but they do need to have all of those foundational skills."

9:30 a.m. — "Freeze!"

Students know what this command means. Most of the class moves to another activity station, and another six students rotate into the small-group math session run by Hickman.

9:32 a.m. — Small-group math

Hickman runs her small group in waves, with students sorted by the sophistication of their math awareness. This group is the most advanced, and she moves quickly from basic shapes — paper cut into circles and rectangles and triangles — to more sophisticated shapes. The students in this group are instant experts at pointing out shapes around the classroom. What's the door? A rectangle. They all get it. Then Hickman brandishes a small, square cardboard box. "This has 1, 2, 3, 4, 5, 6 — six sides. What shape has six sides?" The students seem stumped. "A cube," she answers.

Emily Thomas and some of her classmates listen eagerly to their teacher.

10:26 a.m. — Class gathering

A song led by the teachers: "Everyone find your place on the floor/Not on the ceiling/Not in the door/Everyone find your place on the floor." There's a lesson about the seasons, an announcement about an ice cream social at the end of the day (a popular proclamation), and then Wilder dismisses the students for "Journal," where they talk about their drawings. Louise has drawn a house with a cat peering out the second-floor window. Prompted by Wilder, Louise talks about her cat-and-house scenario, and the teacher-polished dialogue is written by Wilder at the top of the drawing for Louise to see.

10:45 a.m. — Snack

Goldfish and raisins are the main event.

What Makes a Quality Preschool

AppleTree is a rarity, a preschool program that mirrors the famous Perry experiment in both spending and the sophistication of its instruction (the AppleTree curriculum differs from Perry). Although the program, which serves 620 students in seven locations throughout Washington, D.C., is too new to prove its worth over time, as Perry has done, the early indicators are positive. Early childhood expert Craig Ramey, who was part of the early childhood intervention program in North Carolina known as Abecedarian, a successful experiment that rivals Perry in fame, released an evaluation of AppleTree in August 2010. The findings: AppleTree's design equals or improves upon the designs of the best preschools in the country, and the gains among AppleTree students in the school readiness indicators of language, mathematics, and literacy skills match what would be expected from such a high-quality program.

Already, we know that large-scale, high-quality preschools, even if they are not funded on an AppleTree or Perry scale, can have considerable impacts. In 1998, prompted by a lawsuit over school funding inequities, the New Jersey Supreme Court ordered the state to set up high-quality preschools for 3- and 4-year-olds in the highest-poverty districts, known as the Abbott districts. The Abbott track record is more than promising: Poor and minority fourth-graders in New Jersey are more likely to read proficiently than their peers in all but a few states. And there's even better news, writes preschool analyst Sara Mead, who studied the program for the New America Foundation: "... [T]he Abbott districts that have the most aggressively implemented intensive literacy supports at the elementary level, while also aligning pre-K and the early grades, have closed the achievement gap for the disadvantaged and minority students they serve."[1]

Another promising large-scale preschool program can be found in Oklahoma, which offers universal preschool to all 4-year-olds. That strategy appears to have paid off. "The Oklahoma program is producing positive results across multiple measures for the state's children," reported Steve Barnett from the National Institute for Early Education Research at Rutgers University. Barnett's 2005 study revealed vocabulary gains 28 percent higher than the gains of children without the program. That equals an additional three months of progress. The program boosted math skills by 44 percent.

The momentum behind providing high-quality preschool has picked up. Between 2000 and 2010 the enrollment in state programs doubled, said Barnett, with quality rising. Programs such as AppleTree are likely to produce the greatest gains. Aside from the benefits passed along to the 620 students, the importance of programs like AppleTree probably lies in setting examples for other preschool programs to follow.

"We're trying to change the definition of 'quality,'" said AppleTree founder Jack McCarthy. "We want to make sure that 'quality' is defined in terms of outcomes that are aligned with success in school." All the skills that are needed to succeed in school — language, vocabulary, numeracy, attending to instruction, being able to take direction from adults — are carefully plotted out in AppleTree's Every Child Ready program, which is available for others to adopt. "When children have that for two years, they are ready to compete with kids in any ZIP code. We have it within our power to close the achievement gap before children enter kindergarten. Just imagine what that would look like in a city like Washington, what that would do in terms of poverty and crime. It's possible. It can be done. It's just a matter of having the will."

Endnotes

1. Sara Mead, *Education Reform Starts Early* (Washington, DC: New American Foundation, 2009).

First-grade teacher Constance Caruso explains student reading goals to a group of parents in an Academic Parent Teacher Team.

Chapter 8

BUILDING PARENTAL INVOLVEMENT

It's an unusual 53 degrees on a December afternoon in Phoenix, and parents straggle into Constance Caruso's colorful first-grade classroom for English language learners bundled against the cold. Caruso, fresh out of an Arizona State University teacher preparation program, is tall and thin with dark brown hair and a no-nonsense manner. She greets the parents at Larry C. Kennedy Elementary with a quick smile and directs them to manila folders with their children's names on them. To the uninitiated, this evening is shaping up to be like any other parent–teacher meeting, albeit with better attendance.

But for the next hour, Caruso and her students' parents go far beyond the average parent–teacher pleasantries about bake sales, field trips, or student behavior. Instead, they are talking exclusively about student data and goal setting. And not once does anyone look bored. This promising new family engagement model is called Academic Parent Teacher Teams, or APTT. Piloted in Phoenix's Creighton School District, which educates 6,700 students, 92 percent of whom are eligible for free and reduced-price lunch, APTT combines best practices from family engagement research into one teacher-led engagement model. The model clarifies the teacher, student, and parent roles in a child's education. They share specific, parent-friendly information on each student's learning and growth. They provide concrete methods for parents to help at home. They create a school expectation that all adults in a child's life contribute to their education. They break down barriers between parents and teachers, and parents and parents.

This is not family engagement as you know it.

When Caruso has the reading scores of the entire class displayed and is talking about the class goals for the next 60 days, a father named Jorge Armenta raises his hand. Armenta, who has a daughter in third grade and a son in Caruso's class, wants to share his strategies for helping his son with reading at home. "I get a stopwatch out, and I give him a minute" to read as many words as he can, Armenta says. "He gets really excited." This is Armenta's third year participating in Academic Parent Teacher Teams; he began when his daughter was in first grade, and now his son is showing steady progress as a reader. Caruso is unsurprised by the correlation between family participation in the program and student success. To her, the model has an obvious impact on student achievement. After her September meeting, she saw scores improve dramatically. The morning after her December meeting, students excitedly told her they had already worked with their parents on their addition and subtraction cards.

Jorge Armenta's focused comments exemplify the divide between Academic Parent Teacher Teams and the average family engagement program. And that difference, where a father is sharing at-home teaching strategies instead of asking how many brownies he should bring to the bake sale, is exactly what makes the model so promising. The model was invented by Maria Paredes, the former community education director for Creighton, and started as a pilot in a handful of classrooms. It's now in most of the classrooms in Creighton and in a handful of districts from California to Washington, D.C. Paredes has pin-straight brown hair, a straight-talking manner, and none of the bland niceness one might associate with someone who has devoted her life to involving low-income families in education. But with her laser focus on data and student success, Paredes could very well be the new face of family engagement — family engagement that works.

The Engagement Field

Family engagement has proven, time and time again, to be a major predictor of student success. The achievement gap — between the academic performance of low-income students and middle-income students — is often attributed to the fact that middle-income families are more likely to be involved in their child's education. It's not that low-income families don't care or don't value education — focus groups indicate quite the opposite. Instead, research suggests that low-income parents are much more likely to believe they aren't equipped to help their child with academics. They're much more likely to defer to the teacher's authority, and to believe that their involvement is somehow getting in the way (this is especially borne out in the Latino community, where the teacher is seen as an authority and is not to be questioned).

It follows, then, that research indicates that the most effective ways of increasing family engagement among low-income families is simple: have the teacher extend a specific invitation to the parents to get involved. Once parents believe that the teacher's expectation is that they will help, not stay out of the way, they are much more likely to get involved. Their child's achievement rises accordingly. But this type of research hardly sees the light of day in most districts and schools. Family engagement, alternatively described by practitioners as the "ugly stepchild" of school reform, the "fifth wheel," or the "fluffy extra," seems to be the last bastion of the anything-goes approach to education.

In 1998, Paredes first started as community education director in the Creighton School District, which at the time had almost 100 percent of its students qualify for free and reduced-price lunch. Back then, Paredes defined family engagement broadly; she just wanted to get parents into the school. One of her biggest initiatives was organizing classes for parents to increase their own skills in technology, parenting, health, English — you name it. The parents came, up to 600 each semester. Her projects successfully built a welcoming school climate.

Paredes was in good company when she considered success in family engagement to be any program that brings smiling parents into the school. Most family engagement in school districts is based on whatever makes people feel good, not on what impacts student achievement. Backpack donation bucket? Family engagement. Christmas potluck? Family engagement. Canned food drive? Definitely family engagement. Helen Westmoreland, a family engagement researcher and evaluator who left the Harvard Family Research Project to work for the Flamboyan Foundation, which focuses on improving educational outcomes through family engagement, said this attitude is the norm. Part of it, she said, is that parent participation is the easiest thing to measure. It's something you can see, and schools gear their approaches toward any activities that generate a visible parent presence. The focus on turnout for turnout's sake highlights an even bigger problem with most schools' approach to family engagement: a lack of attention paid to the end goal. "A lot of districts and schools have not always taken that hard look in the mirror and said, 'What is it we believe about family engagement, and what should it be in service of?'" Westmoreland said.

For best-practice engagement to spread, family engagement needs to be treated just as seriously as any other highly regarded initiative to improve education. States, nonprofits, districts, and even individual schools need to be willing to invest more in research and development for their staff. Programs and initiatives need to set goals and metrics and track their progress with data. But, at least for now, that focus is lacking. In most districts, family engagement is still a rudderless, low-impact initiative.

Paredes and Westmoreland argue that school-based family engagement is most effective when defined as collaboration between families and teachers with the goal of improving student learning. When engagement is zoomed out from the school to include nonprofits and community-based groups, it can have several other worthwhile goals. Engagement can have an antipoverty bent and emphasize wraparound services for families, a democratic focus that stresses family advocacy and participation in decision making, or a child development emphasis that stresses family–child interactions. All are worthwhile, but most schools don't think through their particular goals and settle for a mushy amalgamation of all four approaches, something school researchers refer to as "random acts of family engagement." Then they measure their program by what they can see: parents showing up in the schools. Parents show up, schools feel happy, it's a win for all!

The acceptance of this feel-good, non-research-based approach to family engagement programs has led to some truly inadequate programming. School-based family coordinators are prime offenders. The New York City Department of Education's parent coordinator initiative, for example, which at its launch in 2003 cost a reported $43 million a year, was designed by then-Chancellor Joel Klein as a path to improve family engagement in schools. A report from the city's public advocate in 2004 found that two-thirds of the coordinators, whose job description included a requirement to be available some nights and weekends, were unreachable after 5 p.m. on their district-provided cell phones. Even more problematic was the fact that 51 percent of the coordinators failed to return a parent phone call within a week.

The second, more systemic problem with family coordinators is that the position outsources engagement to someone who can't possibly know as much about each child's learning and needs as the adult who is with that child eight hours a day: the teacher. "If you want to impact student achievement," Westmoreland said, "the two people who do that are the teacher and the person who is in charge of extending instruction at home, the parent." Paredes's model uses family coordinators, but in a very new way: as facilitators of the relationship between teachers and families. Westmoreland agrees that this model is promising (the Flamboyan Foundation is so impressed with Paredes's impact on Creighton that it's replicating the model in eight Washington, D.C., schools this year and using similar parent coordinator job descriptions). But by and large, family coordinators are around to take family engagement off teachers' plates. Being in favor of family engagement coordinators "is an incredibly political, popular policy position," Westmoreland said. "But, like other aspects of education, it ends up being more of a jobs program than a kids program. Does it help kids learn and do better? I would be interested in seeing that proven."

Family coordinators aren't the only disappointment in family engagement programs. Most everything the average parent or school defines as family engagement — potlucks, fundraisers, generic school newsletters — does not have an impact on student achievement.

It's fair to fault schools and districts for ignoring everything they know about goal setting, metrics, and accountability when it comes to family engagement programs. It's harder to bash them for failing to implement best-practice family engagement programs because, well, there aren't really any. Researchers have proven that family engagement is important, they know what approaches don't seem to work, and they know the kinds of things parents need to know to better help their children. But the "how" — best practices for implementation of programs — don't really exist. "The field has been really underinvested for a very long time," Westmoreland said. With a few exceptions, mostly in the realm of parent-leadership programs that have been proven to result in quantitative student learning improvements, "there's not a really robust research base around specific implementation practices … that says, 'If you do this, you'll impact student achievement.'" Schools and districts committed to improving their family engagement programs for now have to pilot their own best guesses of what works based on a few research studies in the field.

At the same time that districts and states are failing to invest proper resources in ensuring that family engagement practices are effective, some critics opine that engaged families are the only way to improve schools, and it's not the schools' job to try to fill in for absentee parents. This approach is problematic. First, as Academic Parent Teacher Teams prove, this question ultimately circles back to the very place critics say has limited power: the school. Actions by educators at schools can be the difference between involved families and disengaged ones. While a program like APTT is a serious addition to teachers' job descriptions, the Creighton experience indicates that in the long run teachers find their jobs easier because their outreach provides dividends in increased student learning. Second, only highly functioning schools can pull off highly functioning family engagement. As Creighton's assistant superintendent, Jim Bogner, explains it, "You can't walk into a nonfunctioning district and get results from family engagement." Everything has to move at the same time: effective principals to prioritize outreach and recognize its impact, effective teachers who can educate children and build trust with parents, curriculum and instructional practices that work, and effective data systems to provide accessible information for each student.

Why Creighton Worked

What ended up setting Creighton's family engagement work apart from other districts'? First, Creighton was among the few districts that invested in a management-level position responsible solely for engagement: Paredes's role as community

A father reviews material during a meeting of his child's Academic Parent Teacher Team.

education director. Paredes was in on management conversations about students with persistently low scores, and assumed that her office had to produce higher achievement through community education in the same way that a teaching and learning department has to increase learning through educator development. Weren't there family engagement strategies out there that might affect student achievement? She thought that there were.

Paredes's experiment to implement a new kind of family engagement started with the district's parent liaisons, who were paid with federal funds for low-income schools to be in each building. At the time, this position was similar to New York's "parent coordinators." Paredes agreed with the criticisms that the average family coordinator position constitutes "putting out little fires" such as helping parents get to the food bank or the doctor. The families loved them, but were they driving student achievement in the years when learning to read means the difference, 10 years down the line, between dropout and diploma? The data sure weren't promising. So Paredes asked her liaisons to work with the families of the 15 lowest-performing students in kindergarten through second grade. Her mandate was clear: "I told them, 'You are fully responsible for those 15 students and their families. And you are going to help those students learn and get as close to grade level as possible through their families.'" Rossy Vasquez, the liaison at Larry C. Kennedy Elementary School, described the shift as a "shock." But she said Paredes was there every step of the way, arranging for twice-monthly professional development sessions for liaisons to solidify their knowledge of basic skills. By the end of the year, teachers were seeing previously rowdy kids showing up to school on time and ready to learn. The students started doing better on their work, and their parents expressed more confidence in their own ability to help their children. Now Vasquez has no doubt that teaching parents how to ensure their children's academic success is the best possible use of her time. "That's why parents have their kids in school," she said. "Because they want them to be successful."

Reimagining parent liaisons as parent academic coaches was a success, but to reach more families, the program would have to spread. Paredes recruited a dozen teachers willing to convert traditional 15-minute parent–teacher conferences two times a game of war that they can play with their kids to improve addition skills. After a short demonstration by Caruso and her translator, the parents get to practicing. Their heads are down, focusing on their own addition and laughing and celebrating when they win.

By the end of the night, Caruso has shown the parents data on high-frequency words, addition and subtraction skills, and reading fluency. She has given them time to fill in goal sheets for their children (she got them started by writing individual goals for each student, but the parents are responsible for committing to three approaches per subject to help their child reach those goals). They leave with cards and a card game, addition and subtraction flash cards, a packet of short stories, and all of their children's data.

Jenny Lopez, Caruso's colleague and across-the-courtyard neighbor at Kennedy, has been teaching for eight years and holding APTTs in her first-grade classroom for English language learners for the past two years. Helping these children succeed is personal for Lopez: She moved to the United States from El Salvador as a child and attended the same elementary school where she teaches today. (Kennedy legend has the 4' 11" Lopez being scolded during her first year on the job by another teacher to "get in line"; her colleague thought she was still a student.) After teaching two siblings, one before the days of the parent engagement model and one this year, Lopez sees the younger sibling progressing much faster than the older one, from almost last in the class to first, because the parents now have tools and guidance about how to help at home. "At the beginning of my teaching career, I thought all the responsibility fell on me to teach the students," Lopez said. "Now, I share that responsibility."

Creighton families are similarly enthusiastic. Aracley Soriano, whose daughter is in Caruso's class, says there's no question that attending the group conferences changed her behavior. "Because of what [the teachers] taught us, it's easier for me to help my daughter," Soriano said through a translator. "I understand how to help her better, so that she can learn more and improve." She had attended the meeting in Caruso's class the night before and was already using the card game to start helping her daughter add in her head and not on her fingers. Martha Navarro, a mother of three, is a college graduate from Mexico and has always helped her children with schoolwork at home. But she says the meetings have changed her perception of her role by giving her more approaches to help her kids learn. "At the [first meeting of the year], my daughter could only read three words. Only three!" Navarro began reviewing words and reading stories with her daughter. By the next meeting, 60 days later, Navarro's daughter could read 50 words, five more than the goal of 45.

Soriano and Navarro both speak only Spanish, something Navarro admits is a frustration in helping her kids learn to read English at home. But she said there are ways around this: "We have flashcards [from the program], and my children tell me how to pronounce the words. We also have a CD with the pronunciations of frequently used words [that the program gave us]. Using that CD helps me. It's helpful for both me and my children."

Part 4

ACCELERATING ACADEMIC RIGOR

Jillian Taschereau and Carlos Leonardo are taking AP classes as part of a program to expand access to rigorous courses at Methuen High School.

Chapter 9

RISING TO THE CHALLENGE

The morning sunshine streams into the Methuen High School cafeteria. It's just before 9 o'clock on a Monday, too late for breakfast and too early for lunch, yet still the place is packed.

As the marching band practices next door and girls outside the windows perform calisthenics on this unseasonably warm New England fall morning, more than 300 teenagers hunch over circular tables in groups of four and five. They do not have pizza or chocolate milk to command their attention but rather graphing calculators and copies of *King Lear*.

Along the first wall closest to the entrance (and the band music), AP English, history, and foreign language teachers correct papers between individual student consultations. Farther inside, in the second room of the cafeteria, AP math and science teachers are doing the same.

Jillian Taschereau, 16, strategically seats herself in the center for easy access to all of them. She's a junior taking three AP classes — Biology, English Language, and U.S. History — up from none when she was a sophomore.

This period, a 48-minute daily block that Methuen calls AP Enhancement, "saves my life, having all my teachers in one room to calm me down when I'm freaking out," says Jillian, who has a strong swimmer's build, a wavy light-brown ponytail, and a belted gray sweater-dress. She is spending at least 3.5 hours a night on homework now, compared with less than an hour last year. Today she is working on a 19th-century magazine cover for the history class featuring Horace Mann as "Man of the Year" for founding public schools, an article called "How Extreme Is Your Wealth?" on social class division, and news stories on pre–Civil War riots and the women's rights movement, as well as a prelab assignment on diffusion and osmosis for bio.

In years past, Jillian might have just been passed along from one standard-level class to another. Maybe she would have gone to a local college and been fine; maybe she would have needed remedial work. But now she is on a different course, one designed to send her academically prepared to a selective institution of higher education, to make her a valuable contributor to a knowledge-driven workforce. "Some kids automatically get this stuff right away," she said. "I have to work hard for it, but then when you get it, you're like, 'Oh my God, I'm smart. I'm doing what college kids do.'"

The rigor of a student's high school classes has long been the No. 1 factor in college admissions. And the College Board's AP classes have long been the gold standard for challenging high school course work. Also for a long time, though, those classes were the province of an elite group of students and schools. Methuen, the only high school in a modest city of 47,000 in northern Massachusetts, was typical in that it screened students for AP based on grades and required teacher recommendations, interviews, and essays. For 20 years, its AP enrollment was stagnant. In 2009, 74 students in a school of 1,900 — 4 percent — took an AP Exam.

Then along came Morton Orlov II, a retired Army infantry officer who found a second calling in public education. Orlov had taken a gamble leaving his position as principal of Chelsea High School outside Boston to preside over the new Mass Math + Science Initiative. He had six years and a $13 million grant to create a paradigm shift in the commonwealth's high schools. Armed with evidence from a successful program in Dallas, he set out to prove that with the right supports and incentives, vastly more teenagers are capable of college-level work in math, science, and English (in everything, really, but the grant only covers those three subjects). He scoured the state looking for a representative sample of schools to test his hypothesis. He reacted immediately when he saw Methuen's data. Enormous potential was sitting there.

Unearthing Possibility

When he entered the U.S. Army as an 18-year-old from upstate New York, Mort Orlov would have told you he was doing it to jump out of airplanes. But as the years passed and he rose through the ranks, he realized that his greatest thrills came on the ground, training other soldiers. After the terrorist attacks of Sept. 11, 2001, Orlov was a lieutenant colonel preparing for deployment to Iraq or Afghanistan. He'd seen combat before and had no hesitation about serving. But he had conflicting demands back home helping his wife care for their young autistic son. He decided his family had to come first and took a leave. Based in Columbia, S.C., his wife wanted to move to Boston to be near extended family. "I said, 'There's not a lot of jobs for infantry colonels in Boston,'" Orlov recalled. "Like, none." Actually, there was precisely one: a two-year professorship of military science at Boston University, and Orlov was selected for it in 2002.

At BU, Orlov got to know the dean of the school of education, which was helping to run the public schools in Chelsea, a high-poverty district northeast of the city. Around the time Orlov's professorship was ending, the dean sat next to Orlov's wife at a social event and learned that his military retirement was imminent. The next thing Orlov knew, he was being approached about applying for the Chelsea superintendent's job. His wife had worked as a teacher, and Orlov briefly considered joining her in the field, but "I looked at all the regulations [to enter teaching] and said, 'I'm not sure how I'm going to figure that out.'" Yet there he was, a finalist to lead an entire school district. He didn't get that offer. However, they gave him another: to be the principal of Chelsea High. By then he'd been promoted to full colonel and the Army was trying to entice him to stay. "Going into the high school was a major challenge as opposed to going to the next level in an area I knew quite well," said Orlov, now 52. "At some point, you have to move on."

Orlov was lucky in that a predecessor at Chelsea High had done an excellent job getting discipline in order. He saw his most fundamental task as establishing an "academic engine" to get kids from some of the poorest neighborhoods in the state into honors classes. His work impressed the nonprofit Mass Insight Education, which approached him in 2007 as it was applying to get Massachusetts a coveted share of a $125 million grant. The grant, from ExxonMobil to the National Math and Science Initiative, would help six states address the economic threat posed by American students entering college unprepared for rigorous courses and math and science careers. It was inspired by a Dallas program that began paying students and teachers at 10 high-poverty schools for passing AP Exams in 1996 and saw the number of passing scores soar from 29 in 1995 to 664 a dozen years later.

As president of the Mass Math + Science Initiative, Orlov found himself responsible for recruiting a geographically representative sample of schools around the state to buy into a twofold strategy. One, give teachers and students the support they need so that any determined kid can succeed in AP. Two — here would be the rub — pay them for the results. His charge was to vastly improve academic rigor for underrepresented students, with the word "underrepresented" being broadly defined and intentionally so. He would, of course, target low-income and minority students. In 2008, Massachusetts had 12,000 African American high school juniors and seniors, and African Americans accounted for only 65 of the state's passing AP science exams. But Orlov was also looking to get more girls into advanced math and science courses, more boys into advanced English, and more students of every background living up to their potential.

And in Methuen, an awful lot of potential was going untapped. The city is located just south of the New Hampshire border between wealthy North Andover and blue-collar Lawrence, with demographics looking more like Lawrence all the time. A third of the high school's student population is minority, mostly Latino; a third is also low income. The community is tight-knit and committed to doing right by its kids. The school is in the midst of a $100 million renovation to replace its open-air classrooms, an unfortunate fad in 1970s architecture.

Since Orlov first made his case to the administration and faculty, the school has undergone a massive transformation, far beyond what even he envisioned. It released many of the shackles barring AP admission and began encouraging students to enroll based on teacher recommendations and PSAT/NMSQT scores. Counselors now identify promising prospects using the College Board's AP Potential™, a free online tool that predicts the likelihood that a student will pass an AP Exam based on

PSAT/NMSQT performance. They can set the bar as high or as low as they want, and they keep moving it lower. No determined student is turned away.

Methuen went from 59 enrollments in AP math, science, and English courses to 543 — an increase of 820 percent over two years. It blew its five-year target out of the water in the first year alone. The goal was to go from 41 passing, or "qualifying," scores in the three subjects in 2009 to 79 qualifying scores in 2010 and 113 by 2014. Instead, the school hit 141 qualifying scores the first year. The second year, the number was 167. New goal: 226 by 2014.

How did this happen?

Rising to the Occasion

A few years before anyone at Methuen High School had heard of Mort Orlov, a tall girl named Stefanie walked into a teacher's classroom disappointed that her application to take his AP English Literature class had been rejected. The teacher, Bud Jennings, asked her why she wanted to take AP, expecting the standard reply that it would look good on a college application. He clearly remembers her answer on that spring day in 2005: "She said, 'Well, you know, I really do enjoy literature, and I'm more of a math and science student, but it just is interesting to me that there's all this stuff in literature that some people see that I don't immediately see, and I want to learn about that.' That got my attention. I said, 'Look, I'm not the one who makes the decision, but this is what I would suggest. ... You go to my boss, you address her very respectfully and tell her you're gonna really try hard and you want to do it.'"

Jennings's boss is the department coordinator, Ann Marie Krusell, a 37-year veteran of the school who for ages oversaw AP English admissions. "I was sort of dead-set on the process," she said. But Stefanie persisted, and eventually Krusell decided to give her a chance. The AP English Literature class that year was the most academically advanced group that Jennings has taught in nearly two decades. Stefanie never took her place there for granted. "Stefanie was the kid who would come after school and say, 'I really want to be a good writer,'" Jennings said. "She was open to learning about literature in a completely different way." She scored a 4 of 5 possible points on the AP Exam, earning herself college credit.

In Stefanie's honor, the school established the annual Cordelia Award, after the heroine in *King Lear,* for a student who rises to the occasion. So a seed had already been planted when Orlov reached out to Joseph Harb, the science coordinator and designated administrator for AP, in 2008. Orlov explained that the Mass Math + Science Initiative was about to get under way in an initial group of schools, and he was looking for others to apply for year two.

Harb, a local who traded Tufts Medical School for teaching high school biology and coaching football and hockey in the 1990s, asked Orlov to come for a meeting. He invited the school and district administration, the AP teachers, and teachers who might be called upon to teach AP if Methuen signed on. The superintendent at the time, Jeanne Whitten, asked a lot of questions but, once on board, never looked back. The local governing body, called the school committee, voted unanimously in favor.

Even more important was teacher support. "If you're going to be successful, this has to be about teachers stepping up to this new philosophy," Orlov said. "We're all about student outcomes, but this is a teacher-led initiative." Numerous schools that have opened AP classes have seen their programs flounder, or at least take longer to get off the ground, amid teacher resistance. Teachers often are concerned that they'll have to dumb down the material or are wary of extra work. Some at Methuen thought they would be setting students up for failure. "We had this tried-and-true system where departments made it necessarily difficult for a kid to get into an AP course, and the thinking was, 'If it's not broken, don't fix it,'" Jennings said. "I just don't think they were seeing that there were a lot of kids, particularly low-income and minority students, who weren't being represented." Interestingly, none of the opposition came from those actually teaching AP. All of them wanted to expand access. Jennings said they understood that "in fact, the material really would be accessible to a far greater number of kids."

Students and teachers both get a payoff for producing results. Students make $100 per qualifying score in math, science, and English, and teachers get $100 for each qualifying score in their classes. Teachers are also eligible for an award for everyone in a department where kids collectively meet a target. Last year, the average teacher award in the program statewide was $1,741. Methuen's average was $2,231, a reflection of the school's outstanding performance.

Jillian Taschereau chats with Bud Jennings in the cafeteria at Methuen High School, where students have access to all the AP teachers during a daily period to support increased AP participation.

The rewards system did not go over well with the teachers union. In April 2009, just as the program was about to begin, the Methuen Education Association filed a grievance saying that the district had violated its collective bargaining agreement by altering teachers' pay structure and work requirements. The union said incentive money should go to an entire faculty. During an arbitration hearing, the district did something unusual: It called on the AP teachers to testify against their own representatives. The final testimony, from a teacher about to retire, was particularly powerful. "She got up and said, 'I've been teaching for 34 years. I've been involved in a lot, and this is simply the finest program that I've ever seen,'" Orlov said. "It was just a moment of clarity when you realize that if you get past all these adult noises, this program was doing what we said we were going to do, and we were taking care of kids and taking care of teachers in the process."

The district lost the arbitration anyway, but it appealed in Essex County Superior Court. Justice Maynard Kirpalani upheld the validity of the incentives in an April 2011 ruling that gave teachers the freedom to sign independent agreements with the Mass Math + Science Initiative. Orlov can now pay them directly without the district as an intermediary. The union did not take the case further.

'Never Going Back'

The Mass Math + Science Initiative is producing tremendous results not just in Methuen but around the state. Since 2008, the program has resulted in more than 4,000 new enrollments in AP math, science, and English classes, and Massachusetts students have achieved more than 1,000 additional passing scores on AP Exams in those subjects. Last year, the 45 participating high schools produced 51 percent of the state's gains for African American and Hispanic students on AP Exams, and 72 percent of the increase for low-income students.

This year, the initiative has expanded to 53 schools. Just one, in Dedham, faced a union challenge to the teacher incentives at the time of publication. Statewide, teachers were awarded $644,000 last year. Methuen teachers received $29,000, and Methuen students won $16,700 in incentives.

The current Methuen superintendent, Judith Scannell, has continued the administrative backing, worth about $80,000 a year for supplies, substitutes during teacher professional development, and buses for students' regional Saturday study sessions with other participating schools.

Methuen now has an expanded corps of AP teachers who are attending five extra days of professional development during the summers plus two days during the academic year. They are leading the daily AP Enhancement periods (which cover all subjects, not just math, science, and English), sharing best practices with colleagues at other high schools and volunteering to chaperone the Saturday sessions. Methuen is exceeding targets for teacher and student participation on Saturdays. "The high number of teachers arriving on Saturdays for six hours of calculus or six hours of English literature — that is a reflection of teacher dedication," Orlov said. "That leadership will get you the rigor you're looking for. It's democratizing access and saying, 'This hard work that you're doing as students is a good thing, and we're right there with you. We're not just imposing it.'"

The big area where Methuen still needs work is in its minority participation and pass rate. The number of passing scores by Hispanic and African American students in the measured subjects has gone from two to 16, a 700 percent increase but still way too low. Success to Orlov means the demographics of AP classes match the demographics of the school. "That's a tall order," he said, but a handful of Massachusetts schools in his program have achieved it. Not long ago, Bud Jennings had a revealing talk with some bright Hispanic girls who were afraid to take AP. He asked them why they hadn't been in honors courses since ninth grade. "Mr. Jennings, you don't understand Hispanic culture," they told him. "If an eighth-grade teacher makes a suggestion about a class to a Hispanic mother or father, even if the kid wants to try higher, the parent will say, 'Your teacher knows everything.' The white parents, if we're gonna put your kid in a [standard-level] course, they reply, 'Absolutely not, my kid is better than that.'" Jennings said the minority juniors and seniors who are in AP "are doing a good job as role models for younger kids who might see AP as a white endeavor."

Carlos Leonardo, 17, sits quietly in the back row of an AP Physics classroom awaiting renovation, a temporary orange wall blocking the noise and a photocopied picture of Albert Einstein's head taped over the broken clock. Carlos has cropped hair, dark jeans, a red T-shirt, and black Nikes. He puts his head in his hand as he looks over a worksheet on circle circumference and diameter. He is a senior at Methuen who had never taken AP before this year, and now he is in three AP classes: Statistics and Spanish in addition to this one. "My teachers recommended me to take these classes, and I guess they were right," he said sheepishly.

Carlos's friends are in AP classes, but he just didn't see himself as AP material. His junior year Spanish teacher thought otherwise. He was, after all, earning straight A's. Physics, his hardest class, has gotten him thinking about becoming a computer engineer. "I didn't know what I was gonna do after high school," said Carlos, who was in the midst of filling out applications to Boston University and the University of Massachusetts at Amherst and Lowell. "I took this class and I realized I could do something better."

Jillian, who wants to be a forensic scientist, has several friends who aren't in AP. "All my friends make fun of me," she said. "They're like, 'You're such a dork.'" It's a cross she doesn't mind bearing. "If you're taking AP, everyone looks up to you and teachers think of you so differently," she said. Coordinating the Saturday sessions around her swim practices and part-time jobs as a supermarket cashier and baby-sitter is challenging but worth the effort.

Last year's Cordelia Award — a book and a plaque — went to an artistic boy who tried mightily at the beginning of the year to transfer out of AP English Literature, having decided the workload was too much. The school is clear with students and their parents when they sign up for AP that they will not be able to transfer, lest its class schedule be thrown into chaos. So he had to stick it out, and he ended up forming great connections between the literature and the art that is his passion.

The National Math and Science Initiative grant will sunset in 2014. By that time, Orlov hopes the data will be compelling enough across a geographically representative sample of schools to persuade state leaders that the reforms are worth institutionalizing. He's also looking for institutionalization in the cultures of individual schools. In that regard, the work in Methuen is done. "Even if this thing were to end tomorrow, Methuen's never going back," Orlov said. "They have broken the mold."

Joyce Kenner has maintained a tradition of academic excellence during 17 years as principal of Whitney M. Young Magnet High School.

Chapter 10

THE URBAN EXAM SCHOOL

Elementary school was a lonely time for Myia Esper. It's not always easy being smart, and the Chicago girl was often bored and felt out of place at both of the schools where her mom tried enrolling her. A few miles away, on the city's South Side, Trajan Hammonds felt her pain. Night after night, when his dad would ask if he'd learned anything that day, his answer was no. Farther uptown in the quiet Wicker Park neighborhood, Eric Moen liked being at the top of his class, but his educational options would be limited as he got older since his parents couldn't afford to send him to a private school. Then a few years ago, these three kids found letters in their mailboxes that would change the course of their lives. They had been admitted to Whitney M. Young Magnet High School.

Located in the Windy City's Near West Side, Whitney Young is one of the rare public schools in the United States that looks like the dream achieved. The student body is a near-even balance of white, black, Hispanic, and Asian, all of whom routinely go on to the top colleges in the nation. Low-income and middle-class parents send their children to school alongside children of the rich and sometimes even the famous. Despite wildly different ethnic and economic backgrounds, the 2,178 students at Whitney Young all have something in common: above-average intelligence. "I really, really needed this opportunity because I was getting in, like, a rut," said Myia, 14, who displays her penchant for fashion with a gold beret, a trendy brown handbag, and light-pink nail polish. "I felt that if I could get an A just doing half the assignment, I'd be fine. Here I feel I have to do the assignment perfectly. ... Having the smarter students I feel I have to try harder and make sure I'm always at my best."

Urban exam schools like Whitney Young illustrate what's possible in terms of academic rigor, making the best possible education accessible to anyone who meets the entrance criteria. They provide academic excellence to families of modest means that rich parents can get by sending their kids to Choate or Exeter for $45,000 a year. They initiate a leveling process critical to what we perceive as the American Dream. That dream that may not always prove itself in reality, but exam schools are nonetheless a lifeline. "We're not an elite school. We're providing an elite education to the city," said Lynne Mooney Teta, the headmaster of Boston Latin School. "That's really the beauty of our work, giving the students who have the drive and have the ability but don't have the resources a very rigorous education. It is like the American Dream. Families without resources use what we provide them to make a better life for themselves." Exam schools also keep affluent families engaged in public school systems in cities where they would otherwise opt for private schools or flee for the suburbs.

These institutions are community legends, giving younger children something to aspire to, and the competition to get in is fierce. Whitney Young's academic decathlon team has won the Illinois state championship 25 of the past 26 years. In the most recent *Chicago Tribune* rankings of high schools throughout the metropolitan area, Whitney Young was topped only by Northside College Prep, another of the city's public exam schools. (Northside won the decathlon in 2003.) New York City's Stuyvesant High had more semifinalists in the Intel Science Talent Search this year than any other school in the nation. It is one of only four high schools in the world that has produced more than four Nobel laureates. One of the other three is its famous competitor, Bronx High School of Science.

Like Stuyvesant and Bronx Science, many of the country's top magnet schools for gifted students have a science and math focus, producing graduates with the skills needed to fuel the economy. Thomas Jefferson High School for Science and Technology in Northern Virginia is often cited as the top public high school in the United States. From North Carolina to Oklahoma, a growing number of governors have created exam-based public boarding schools to bring together the best and brightest from around their respective states. While that's a relatively new concept, the history of exam schools dates back to 1635, when Boston Latin was founded as the first public school in the United States. Legend has it that nearby Harvard, founded in 1636, was established as a college for Boston Latin's first graduates; the high school still sends a steady stream of alumni there.

Chicago now has nine public high schools with testing criteria, but the demand still far exceeds the supply, demonstrating the widespread desire among students and parents for more rigorous public options. Every year, more than 10,000 students apply for 350 ninth-grade spots at Whitney Young. Another 7,000 apply to be among the 150 admitted as seventh-graders as Myia, Trajan, and Eric were; the school runs a special program for kids ready for high-school-level work two years early. "There's no doubt in my mind that applying to the selective enrollment high schools is more competitive, more stressful than applying to college because you'll get into college somewhere," said Elizabeth Posner, whose daughter is a junior at Whitney Young. "You might not get into a selective enrollment school."

Unfortunately, the admissions process illustrates the inequities in feeder elementary and middle schools. Students who haven't had the kind of opportunities we've described earlier in the book — from a high-quality preschool education to a relay of great teachers throughout their formative years — are far less likely to get in. Those whose parents don't know how to be effective advocates might not even be aware that the opportunity exists, much less enroll them in an exam-prep course. In far-from-perfect systems, exam schools are still providing extraordinary opportunities to many students who wouldn't otherwise have them. They still hold the promise of the achievable dream, and they illustrate why the strategies we are advocating in this book will be vital to get there.

Similarity amid Difference

Whitney Young opened as Chicago's first public magnet school in 1975 on a lot burned during the riots following Martin Luther King Jr.'s assassination. It was named after Whitney Moore

Young, a civil rights leader who had died a few years earlier. Michelle Obama graduated from the school in 1981 and went on to Princeton University. Another tall, strong, and striking African American woman, Joyce Kenner, arrived as an assistant principal in 1990; she has led the school as principal for the past 17 years. A former cheerleader who started out as a physical education teacher in her native Ohio, Kenner moved to Chicago to be the education director at Jesse Jackson's Operation PUSH. Ask her what makes Whitney Young such a success, and she answers unequivocally: "The diversity of our student body and, to some degree, of our faculty. You have students from all walks of life coming together to thrive in this environment despite socioeconomic differences. Michael Jordan's children, two of his three children graduated from Whitney Young. Then you have very, very indigent students here who are able to thrive, too. They are intellectually capable. We have promoted that for all of these years that we've been in the business."

Chicago's selective enrollment high schools admit students based on their seventh-grade grades as well as their scores on an entrance exam. For years, Kenner was able to select the top performers from each racial subgroup to give the school a near-perfect balance. The current district policy allows her less latitude but uses a formula giving an advantage to students from low-income neighborhoods. Kenner does still have discretion over 5 percent of admissions and said she tries to use those slots to keep the school as racially diverse as possible. These so-called principal picks have been the subject of numerous legal inquiries and challenges. Kenner found herself subpoenaed by the FBI a few years ago amid allegations of elected officials seeking favor for particular kids. Many exam schools have done away with hotly contested affirmative action policies. Regardless of what practice is adopted, the clamoring over admissions underscores the need for systemic reforms so that families don't have to view magnet schools for the gifted as their only good option. "Admissions for me just highlighted the need for other fabulous schools because there are so many great, great students who just get a B ... and they would miss the cutoff by three points," said Whitney Young's former admissions director, Lynn Zalon, who now serves as dean of students. "That part was gut-wrenching, letting a parent know that, 'Sorry, your student didn't get in.'"

Admissions isn't the only part of exam schools operating in a fishbowl. Principals can expect pretty much all of their decisions to come under intense parent and community scrutiny. Concerned about grade inflation, Kenner decided last year to establish a schoolwide grading scale where the cutoff for an A is 93, a B is 85, a C is 75, and a D is 68. Parents were less than pleased. "A 60 for a passing grade to me is way too low," Kenner said. "Everybody is not happy about that... Everybody wants an advantage so their child can get into the appropriate [college]." One mom said the grading scale makes her daughter "unnecessarily nuts." The school sprawls out over three buildings (the three A's: academics, arts, and athletics) connected by a skywalk; Kenner communicates with her administration via walkie-talkie. A *Chicago Sun-Times* headline framed in the front office proclaims "Scholastics No. 1 at Young," but there's also a lot of emphasis on the other two A's, particularly the arts. Whitney Young has the only guitar program in Chicago Public Schools, a chamber music camp, and an orchestra room where students arrange for private lessons. The wind ensemble performed at Carnegie Hall in New York City this winter, and 180 kids stay after school to participate in drama.

One of them is 13-year-old Eric Moen, who is on a set crew and also plays guitar and founded a ukulele club. A year and a half into his Whitney Young experience, he's hitting his stride now as an eighth-grader after an overwhelming beginning. He said he felt a "big rush of relief" when he learned he would be able to join his older brother, now a junior, at the school, but then he had a lot to live up to. "I was so used to the fact that I was at the top of the class," said Eric, a loquacious boy with light brown hair and braces, son of a civil engineer and an interior designer who are deeply invested in his education, love city living, and can't afford private school. "Mr. Edwards, my social studies teacher last year, said I used to be the best in the class, but now I'm in a class full of the best of the classes.... Once I was told that statement, I was like, 'Okay, this is for the better-ish.'" As with many exam school students, the highest expectations are the ones he sets for himself. Over time, Eric said, "the feeling of being overwhelmed with all those smart people, it's kind of bubbling down to a point where it's okay.... I have a moral code. I have to meet certain standards that are set."

Eric takes honors biology with Trajan and Myia, where they are studying protein synthesis on the day we visit. Their teacher, Lynne Muhammad, sent her now-grown children to Whitney Young. Trajan, who recently took the ACT three years early and scored a 28 out of 36, once took it upon himself to go through the yearbook and break down his grade by race. "So, yeah. It's pretty diverse," he says in that typically teenage nonchalant sort of way as he chats with Eric and Myia after class. (Eric is white; Trajan and Myia are black.) Eric chimes in: "Mostly at my old school, it was white and black. Here there's a whole horde of different races that I wasn't so used to.... There are some people here who are pretty rich, and there's some people here who aren't so rich." But, he adds, "everybody's smart. We're all different, but that's the one similarity."

Meritocracy in Action

Eight hundred miles east, where almost all the major New York City subway lines converge within a few blocks of each other, sits a high school building unlike any other. Stuyvesant High School, founded in 1904 and for years a beacon of hope for many immigrant Jewish families, moved in 1992 from Manhattan's Lower East Side to a new $150 million facility in Battery Park City, a quarter-mile from the World Trade Center. It sits on the bank of the Hudson River, with views of the New Jersey skyline. In addition to the usual amenities that many public schools covet, from central air conditioning to an indoor pool, the building contains a public art project that makes it a tourist attraction. Embedded randomly throughout its walls are 400 glass blocks. Most are filled with relics, from a chunk of the Great Wall of China to a button from the Revolutionary War, but enough are empty so that each graduating class through 2080 can leave behind a piece of itself. The building's 10 floors are organized by subject area, with the sciences not accidentally occupying most of the top. Stuyvesant was evacuated during the terrorist attacks of Sept. 11, 2001, and for three weeks after, students attended classes at night at a school in Brooklyn while their campus served as an operations base for rescue workers.

Every year, the public and the media watch to see who will earn a spot at this academic powerhouse and New York City icon. A 1972 state law requires that a student's score on the entrance exam be used as the sole criterion for admission to New York City's eight

Trajan Hammonds, Eric Moen, and Myia Esper — pictured with their biology teacher, Lynne Muhammad — are grateful for the opportunity to attend Whitney M. Young Magnet High School.

specialized high schools, among which Stuyvesant has the highest cutoff. The result is that Stuyvesant is 72 percent Asian and 45 percent low-income — the majority of students commute to lower Manhattan from Queens and Brooklyn — but just 3.5 percent black and Hispanic. This year, the city reversed a longstanding decline in the number of underrepresented minorities testing into the eight specialized schools. Black students were offered 6 percent of the slots in 2012 and Latinos 8 percent, a 14 percent increase from 2011. Clearly, the numbers are still far from representative. "I'm one of only a few Latinos in my grade, and I find that disturbing because that does not reflect the demographics of this city in any way, shape, or form," said Alex Carrillo, 17, a Stuyvesant senior who was accepted early to Yale.

Giving a tour of the robotics lab where he is president of the software engineering division on the renowned team, Alex has deep concern in his large, genuine eyes when asked about the opportunities he's received there, though he's quick to point out that the school has been wonderful for him. A thin boy, with thick dark hair, he speaks eloquently about the advantage he had in the admissions process to Stuy, as the school is often called: His parents, an immigrant and a first-generation American who both rose out of poverty to become doctors, signed him up for an expensive course to prepare him for the entrance exam. "The way people get into this school is by having parents who motivate their children to go through very rigorous testing," he says. "I didn't come through on my own; it was my parents who really taught me the importance of working hard and being the best at what I could be. Certainly not all families are providing that for their children. It's very cultural. There's a circumstance here where not all cultures understand the system. You will definitely find many, many families in the city who don't understand the specialized high school process, where on the other hand, you'll find families who have been preparing their children since preschool to take this test."

Stuy's black and Hispanic students take monthly trips with the parent coordinator to speak about the admissions process at high-poverty, largely minority middle schools. For many years, Stuy brought in black and Hispanic middle school students on afternoons and weekends to prepare them for the entrance exam, but it wasn't enough to make up for what sometimes was years of inadequate schooling. The numbers didn't budge, and the program had to be restructured amid a court challenge. The city education department halted the effort to reevaluate and is preparing to launch a new version. To truly level the playing field, the city must provide rigorous work to children from the time they enter school, with all the reforms that entails, and educate their parents on the magnet exam process years in advance. Another interesting dilemma is that the black and Hispanic students who do have the preparation to test into Stuyvesant are also in high demand at the top private schools, which lure them with full scholarships.

Stuyvesant has some selling points that private schools don't. For example, Principal Stanley Teitel doesn't know of any private school with his breadth of courses, which include every AP subject the College Board offers and popular literature classes like one called "Great Books" to complement the heavy science, math, and technology offerings. Stuy's building is certainly another big check in its favor, but overcrowded classes and insufficient funding are reminders that, yes, this is still a public school. Exam schools typically get less funding per pupil than neighborhood schools because they have fewer students with special needs. Some have alumni endowments to make up the difference, but Stuy does not. Parents and students themselves fundraise for a number of the extracurricular activities. Last year, the school received extra federal funding as a designated Title 1 school, or one serving a high-poverty population, when the federal government temporarily lowered the percentage of students needed to qualify as part of the stimulus package.

Teitel was a longtime science teacher at Stuy before becoming principal in 1999. Behind his gruff New Yorker persona is clearly someone who cares deeply about "the children," as he calls his 3,291 charges. He still teaches a daily section of ninth-grade physics, where he doles out tough love doing unannounced notebook inspections and cold-calling on students to solve problems on the board. ("If I'm going to call myself the instructional leader of this school," he asks, "how can I say that if I don't provide instruction myself?") Teitel is proud of the school's position as one of the founding members of the National Consortium for Specialized Secondary Schools of Mathematics, Science, and Technology. He regularly visits the other schools to get ideas; at the time of our interview, he was looking into ways to increase scientific research opportunities for underclassmen. The Intel competition is only open to seniors, and in preparation at least 10 percent of juniors engage in independent research projects, often using college and university labs. Teitel gives a long creative leash to his faculty, many of whom are top academics in their respective fields, but he is very picky about who gets hired in the rare event of an opening. "Finding people who can provide that level of instruction where the children can understand it is a real challenge," he said. "Just because you have a doctorate in front of your name doesn't mean you can give the children the information."

The Stuyvesant administration goes to great lengths to engage its low-income Asian parents, translating a weekly newsletter into Chinese and Korean and providing interpreters to make them feel comfortable visiting. Students who travel long distances seem truly grateful for the chance to be there. "I really appreciate this school giving me so many opportunities," said Jia Hu, 16, a junior who commutes from Coney Island at the southern tip of Brooklyn. The biggest safety concern at Stuy, as at all the exam schools we visited, is students traveling to and from geographically disparate locations. Despite tough budgetary times, the administration has dedicated 12 guidance counselors (beyond three college counselors) to nurture students' social and emotional well-being in such an intense, fast-paced environment. "If you're bright, committed, and enjoy learning, you're with other kids at your level," said Harvey Blumm, Stuy's parent coordinator. "I tell them it's like playing basketball. If you play against other good athletes, it's going to raise the level of your game. You don't have to worry about being a nerd or being embarrassed because you love school."

Achieving the Dream

If you were to imagine a school that has achieved the dream as Martin Luther King Jr. envisioned it, you might imagine Eleanor Roosevelt High School. Located in Greenbelt, Md., (the "belt" refers to the Washington Beltway to its southwest), Roosevelt enrolls 2,700 students. Sixty-two percent are black, 16 percent are white, 11 percent are Asian, and 11 percent are Latino. Students of seemingly every conceivable nationality, from close to 30 different countries, are in classes side by side and thriving.

Roosevelt is an exam school with a twist. A third of the student body is admitted through a highly selective regional magnet program that, like Stuy, emphasizes science and technology. About 1,700 students a year apply for 225 slots in the Roosevelt Science and Tech program. The other two-thirds of the students are neighborhood kids attending their zoned high school. While Roosevelt isn't quite in the same academic league as Stuy, it demonstrates the potential of translating the exam school culture to a broader population. It is a place where smart is cool, the slackers are pressured by their peers to shape up, and the atmosphere is one of pride.

Last year, Roosevelt had more African American students pass at least one AP Exam than any other school in the country. It had seven National Merit Scholars, seven National Achievement Scholarship winners and seven National Hispanic Scholars. It produces more engineering majors at the University of Maryland than any other high school in the state. Reginald McNeill, who came on as an assistant principal in 1997 and has led the school since 2007, is just the third principal in 15 years. Many staff members send their own children to Roosevelt; McNeill's son graduated in 2010. Google co-founder Sergey Brin is an alum.

Roosevelt's nearly 100 after-school clubs range from the KnitWits (knitting) to Do Something (philanthropy) to recycling to step dancing, from the Asian Student Association to the South Asian Student Association to the Latin, Japanese, and French honor societies. Students pass through the halls in an orderly fashion, and incidents of violence are rare. Administrators do worry about one consistent behavioral problem: parents lying about their home addresses to get their kids admitted. Roosevelt has a Science and Tech–like program for about 80 neighborhood kids a year. Unlike Science and Tech, it has no admissions exam, but students do need to apply and attend a two-week summer program. Though the school technically operates on an eight-period day, 110 students a day come in for "zero period" from 7:15 to 8 a.m. to fit in an extra AP class.

Prince George's County is home to one of the largest middle-class African American populations in the United States. Still, 35 percent of Roosevelt students receive free or reduced-price lunch. The school's building was constructed in the mid-1970s in an ill-conceived attempt at energy efficiency involving virtually no windows, and students jokingly call it a prison. "People say you have to have a brand new building, all kinds of materials," said Assistant Principal Cynthia Thomas. "We don't have any of those things." Roosevelt is proof that neither a sizable low-income population nor lack of fancy resources can trump the power of high expectations. All students are exposed to rigorous work from the moment they walk in the door. "If you're my student, I'm going to push your thinking," AP Government teacher Kenneth Bernstein tells a class of freshmen who are his prospective students on a rainy afternoon last November. "You'll be better able to communicate in writing and verbally what you believe, and hopefully you'll learn how to disagree with people without being disagreeable, taking apart their arguments but not taking apart them. In the process I may create my own worst nightmare: an articulate, persuasive advocate of a position I abhor" — his voice is rising — "in which case I've done my job as a teacher because my job as a teacher is to empower you."

Even more than intelligence, success at an exam school requires perseverance. Roosevelt graduates routinely report back that college seems easy in comparison. At Stuyvesant, two boys creating a computer game called "Stuy-opoly" in an AP Computer Science class replace dollars as the currency with sleep. (Principal Teitel quips that students can have two of the three: good grades, sleep, or a social life.) At press time, Whitney Young was opposing its inclusion in a new citywide proposal to extend the school day and working with city officials to maintain its flexibility in scheduling. While more instructional minutes would be good for most kids in Chicago, Principal Kenner said, her building is already open for extracurricular activities until 11 o'clock at night.

What Money Can't Buy

The extended school day proposal is stressing out many of the 70 parents gathered in the spacious Whitney Young library on a mild Thursday in early February. They are attending a meeting in the school's "Hot Topics" series, where parents bring in experts to educate them on everything from teenage mental health to the subject of today's agenda: developing your child's class schedule. The school is scheduling now for September, seven months away.

Norma Chinn, the guidance department chair, fields questions about foreign language courses. No, students don't get credit for what they test out of. Yes, they can take two languages at once. The options are Spanish, Spanish for Native Speakers, French, Mandarin, Japanese, Italian, Latin, and American Sign Language. Chinn, a brunette with a sleek black shirt and gray skirt, tells the parents that if their children are taking more than two AP classes, they should "catch a break" with at least one class that's not as demanding, particularly if they are going to add an extra class to the day. Okay, but what classes would help them to write a good college essay? Creative writing, Chinn replies, but all English teachers and the writing center are available to help, and she strongly recommends that they do a draft the summer before senior year. Elizabeth Blinderman, whose son is a senior and daughter is a freshman, discusses the importance of thoroughly reading the course catalog. "We've created our own Excel spreadsheet," Blinderman says of her family's personal strategy. "I've found that sort of a handy resource."

This is what it looks like to have parents effectively engaged as advocates for their children. They knew what it took to get their kids into Whitney Young, and now they're learning how to help maintain their success. A dozen of them stay after the meeting to speak with us about what a Whitney Young opportunity has meant to them and their children.

Sharlene Holly has glowing reviews of her daughter's Whitney Young experience, but the University of Chicago administrator is worried about her son, a sixth-grader trying to test in. It's been his goal since his sister was admitted three years ago at the age he is now. "It will be great if he gets in, and it will be a really big challenge if he doesn't because he's been looking forward to it for so long," Holly says. "While Whitney Young is stellar... it isn't solving the overall education problem."

"It does, however, give people an option," Elizabeth Posner chimes in. "It's a very unique model in an urban setting ... where people from all over the city can have the opportunity to get the best education possible."

Helping to organize the Hot Topics series is one of the ways Beth Ann Bryant-Richards gives back to Whitney Young. She felt she'd received a gift when her son tested in. "It was sort of like winning the lottery because then we knew, my husband

and I knew that we did not have to pay $40,000 for four years of private high school," says Bryant-Richards, a freelance writer and writing instructor. "That would have been the only other option that was available to us." Her husband, a lieutenant for the Chicago Police Department, is required to live within city limits, so moving to the suburbs wasn't a choice. "It's a wonderful school," she continues. "Our son is crazy happy here. It's the perfect fit for him, but it saved us a lot of money. It's a great option for middle-income people."

"It's the best education that money can't buy," adds Posner, who is a sales and marketing consultant.

Julia Spearman, a nurse's assistant, has two kids enrolled at Whitney Young and a son who graduated two years ago. "My husband's African American and I'm Hispanic. It was very important for us to find a school that has that diversity, and this is the one," says Spearman, who is president of Whitney Young's local school council, an elected body at all Chicago public schools whose responsibilities include hiring and evaluating the principal and allocating resources. "You get the whole enchilada here. You get your academics, your sports, and stuff you didn't even ask for." Her children surprised her with their desire to learn about other cultures. Her older son joined the Asian Club and learned Asian dance. Though she speaks fluent Spanish and her husband speaks French, her sons signed up for Mandarin and Japanese. "I'm like, 'Easy A. Take Spanish,'" she said. "They're like, 'But I want to challenge myself.'"

Ann-Marie Greenberg, the general manager for a music house, is in a similar predicament as Holly. Her daughter is in eighth grade and loving Whitney Young. Her son is in seventh grade, hoping to get admitted to begin as a freshman. "Just the pressure of not knowing and not having enough spots available for these kids, it's really hard," she says. What will she do if he doesn't get in? Greenberg laughs nervously. "He is a little bit of a chess savant person, so maybe there's some private school that would take him on scholarship. You know, I don't know. There's the Illinois [Mathematics and Science Academy]. That would be a good option, but that doesn't start until sophomore year. And that's a boarding school, and I don't know if I could handle that. The options are so limiting, and that makes people leave the city. But I love Whitney Young so much."

Part 5

PUTTING IT ALL TOGETHER

Chris Steinhauser, a product of Long Beach schools, guides the steady-as-you-go reforms in that city.

Chapter 11

A PERPETUALLY IMPROVING DISTRICT

All too often, you can look at a few facts about a school district — its poverty rate, its minority enrollment — and predict with dismaying accuracy the life trajectory of many of its students. In high-poverty, high-minority (especially African American and Hispanic) districts, students are less likely to enter ninth grade ready for high-school-level classes, less likely to take college-preparation classes, less likely to graduate, and less likely to go on to college. If they do enroll in college, they are less likely to actually earn a diploma. In an ideal world where all students were offered an equal opportunity for a shot at the American Dream, this kind of prediction would not be possible. But in the real world, in the United States, it is reality.

However, there are exceptions — important exceptions offering important lessons.

Consider two districts in California: Long Beach and Fresno. On the surface, they look like mirror images. With nearly 85,000 students, Long Beach is the third-largest school district in the state. Fresno, with 75,000 students, is the fourth largest. Fresno has a slightly higher Hispanic population (62 percent vs. 53 percent) and Long Beach has a slightly higher African American population (16 percent vs. 10 percent). Each district has sizable "other" minority populations, with Fresno home to a large Hmong community and Long Beach home to a sizable Cambodian community. Each district translates its school materials into either Hmong or Cambodian. Fresno's students are slightly poorer than the students in Long Beach (82 percent free and reduced-price lunch vs. 70 percent), but the difference is not enough to expect different school outcomes.

Everything you just read about Fresno and Long Beach would lead an education researcher to assume that students in the two districts would have mirror outcomes. They don't. Let's start with the most important data point: college enrollment. Like it or not, college — at least some college — has become the new high school. In today's economy, some kind of postsecondary training or college is needed for almost any decent-paying job. In Long Beach, nearly 80 percent of the students enroll in a two- or four-year college program. In Fresno, only 59 percent do.[1]

Why the Difference?

Explaining how high school seniors perform in school, and especially how their performance relates to the likelihood that they will go on to college, requires some reverse engineering. What sends Long Beach students on their different trajectory? Take math, for example. In fifth grade, 70 percent of Long Beach students score at or above the proficient level on the California math exams, compared with 56 percent of Fresno students. That math difference persists. In eighth grade, 55 percent of Long Beach students take Algebra I, compared with 43 percent of Fresno eighth-graders. And that, of course, explains the test score differences in eighth grade, where 64 percent of Long Beach students score proficient or above in algebra, compared with 38 percent of Fresno students.

As stark as these numbers look, they were even starker in 2008 when Long Beach and Fresno formed a partnership to learn from one another. At that time, only 40 percent of Fresno fifth-graders scored proficient in math (making the jump to 56 percent today nothing short of extraordinary). The same holds true with eighth-grade algebra participation, which rose from 26 percent to 43 percent in Fresno. And the eighth-grade algebra proficiency rate at Long Beach rose from 38 percent to the current 55 percent. The collaboration with Long Beach was not the only reason Fresno students began doing better, but it was a player, which raises the question: What does Long Beach have to teach Fresno (and other struggling urban school districts)? The answer: Plenty. Successful urban school districts such as Long Beach, Aldine in Texas, and Charlotte-Mecklenburg in North Carolina don't disprove gravitational laws revolving around the negative pull of poverty,[2] but the track records at these districts demonstrate that poverty need not be the sole predictor of destiny.[3]

The Equity Rule

A few basic principles drive day-to-day practices in Long Beach, starting with equity. Most school districts view equity as trying to provide equal or better resources to the neediest schools. Usually, they fail. Those schools in the poor neighborhoods are usually shabbier and staffed by less-capable teachers with lower expectations. To compensate, teachers often resort to grade inflation, which nearly always backfires. In Long Beach, a different story plays out. Consider two elementary schools, Minnie Gant and Lafayette. Gant, located in an affluent neighborhood of Long Beach, would seem to have it all. Students there have always performed well. Lafayette Elementary, by contrast, draws students from a high-poverty neighborhood where nearly half the students speak English as their second language. Based on demographics, you would expect Gant to do well on California's Academic Performance Index (API), which rates schools on a scale from 200 to 1,000 based on standardized test scores. And Gant students are high scorers, averaging 900. Just as predictably, you would expect Lafayette to score around 625, a typical score for a high-poverty elementary school in nearby Los Angeles, for example. But instead, Lafayette scores at 864, nearly as high as Gant.

This is no quirk. Long Beach is full of high-poverty schools rivaling schools in middle-class neighborhoods. How does that happen?

The Long Beach story starts with a catalyst: the gradual decline of the shipyards there and the disappearance of high-paying manufacturing jobs, a process that played out through the 1980s. The city that once was home to a Navy base and a McDonnell Douglas aircraft manufacturing plant got stripped of its economic base. What was once a nearly all-white, middle-class city quickly became a high-poverty, high-minority city, with most of the newcomers Mexican Americans or Cambodians. For a community that always regarded itself as an "Iowa by the sea," these were huge changes. Community leaders drawn together to deal with the dramatic changes came to a consensus: The future of Long Beach would lie in the education of its students. The school reform efforts in Long Beach began with the basics, such as requiring school uniforms — in 1992, Long Beach became the first school district in the nation to do so — and consolidating reading programs, a process that led to the district's adoption of the phonics-heavy Open Court, a program still used today (with considerable supplements).

A Breakthrough in Math

Soon, the Long Beach reforms turned toward greater sophistication, especially in the district math programs. The spark came from math teacher Si Swun, who drew on his familiarity with the highly regarded Singapore Math program to build an elementary math program called MAP^{2}D (Math Achievement Program & Professional Development). The program pulls together the best practices of collaborative learning, heterogeneous grouping (so students learn from one another), and public presentation (valuable to newcomers to speaking English, such as Swun at the time).

Launched in five low-performing schools in 2004-05, the program immediately raised math scores. Since then, MAP^{2}D has spread throughout the Long Beach system, giving elementary math classes a signature feel. Teachers introduce a new math concept using an overhead projector. Then students work on solving similar problems in small groups, reaching a consensus on the math principle behind the problem. Finally, the teacher chooses one student to present. The process sounds deceptively simple, but it requires layers of professional development and coaching to achieve the goal of getting students to truly understand math concepts — a world away from usual math instruction, where students are asked to memorize problem-solving techniques.

In Long Beach, how the math program was launched and expanded is as important as the innovative program itself: Start with the highest-need schools, provide drenching professional development, and then look for ways to capitalize on those elementary school math gains. The key to it all is continuous improvement, which means focusing on the basics, the exacting way MAP²D gets presented to students, while working to wring similar gains out of middle schools. These are among the many reasons Gant and Lafayette elementary schools produce similar scores despite their steep socioeconomic differences — and the reasons for the higher-than-expected college-going rates.

It would be a mistake to conclude that Long Beach schools succeed because of a collection of successful innovations such as the math program. Rather, MAP²D works because it is wrapped inside the systemwide reforms Long Beach has been working on since the 1990s: a focus on key standards, ongoing assessments, collaborative learning, differentiation, structured coaching, regular professional development, and more. All school districts have standout schools; Long Beach works as an entire school district — an important distinction, which is what makes Long Beach special.

Overseeing the district's continuous improvement strategy is Superintendent Chris Steinhauser, who grew up in Long Beach, attended the public schools there, worked as a student teacher in the district, and earned his leadership credentials as principal of Signal Hill Elementary, a school that regularly tops California's list of high-poverty, high-performing schools. Steinhauser, 53, has an "Iowa by the sea" appearance and demeanor — a round-faced, friendly smile and a subdued voice — and comes off more like a small-town Rotarian than a hard-charging urban schools chief. But don't be fooled by the affability. Traces of his intensity are everywhere. He knows everyone is watching what happens in his district, and he's not about to let any school gains lapse while he's superintendent.

Near-equal school outcomes such as those of Gant and Lafayette, despite their stark differences in demographics, are the goal. "It happens through the common professional development we provide everyone, plus the common standards of expectation," Steinhauser said. For example, Long Beach schools are not allowed to set their own grading practices. In many urban districts, students get handed high grades based on low standards, a practice that triggers unwelcome results when students graduate with top GPAs and then fall short on college placement tests, forcing them into remedial courses that are not credit-bearing (see Chapter 13).

At Long Beach, students can't earn a proficient grade in reading unless they achieve a proficient score on their Open Court tests — a threshold that's the same at all schools, including Gant and Lafayette. "So if I am retaining a kid at Gant," Steinhauser said, "that same kid would be retained at Lafayette. That has all been taken out of the control of the schools and is 100 percent consistent." Making sure students at Lafayette stay up with students from wealthier neighborhoods, however, requires pushing more resources to schools such as Lafayette. "We believe kids in school who need more support are going to get more resources, and that is what we do," he said.

The primary resource Steinhauser has to offer is a teacher corps known for both its expertise and esprit de corps. Most Long Beach teachers get recruited directly from California State University, Long Beach, where school district officials teach courses and get to pick who gets the opportunity to student-teach in their schools. Out of that pool come the new hires, who are watched carefully in their first two years, in part because California sets tenure at the two-year mark. "From day one, what is important to me as a school district [superintendent] is to make those teachers high quality. If they are not, what we have to do is get rid of them. We are very good about releasing teachers. We have to make a decision very early on whether someone is going to get tenure. We have to be very conservative in who is going to stay and not going to stay." About a fifth get fired. "There's a certain percentage of that group that I feel bad about because, to be honest, I think some of them would be very good teachers if they had another year to develop. But if we make a mistake, then it is a two-year process to get rid of them that costs $250,000."

Promotions to school leadership spots almost always come internally. "Understanding the culture of our system is very important," Steinhauser said. "Plus, we want to see you in action." During our visit to Long Beach, Steinhauser could only name two principals brought in from outside the district. When outsiders do win jobs in Long Beach, they usually start out in lower positions.

The superior quality of its staff explains how Long Beach appears to be surviving cutbacks that would devastate most school districts. Due mostly to dramatic reductions in state funding, the Long Beach budget fell by $330 million between 2008 and 2011,

Chris Steinhauser makes sure that all school improvements in Long Beach have mechanisms built in for continuous improvement.

leading to 574 layoffs. At high-performing schools, class sizes rose from 25 students to 30. At low-performing schools, the increase was 20 to 30, and the layoffs still hit many of the low-performing schools the hardest. Several of those schools lost as much as 40 percent of their staff.

As of the winter of 2011, there was no evidence of academic setbacks from the layoffs. Hardships, yes. Frantic juggling by principals, yes. But no slackening in student learning. In part, that's because Long Beach schools were designed around a students-first concept.[4] For the most part, the teaching staff at Long Beach is just that much better, that much more dedicated. "I had teachers who were laid off calling in to see how their students did on state tests," Steinhauser said. "The level of professionalism in this district is incredible." Because of the depth of the high-quality-teacher bench in Long Beach, students are less likely to suffer when, due to layoffs, principals are forced to bring in a teacher from another school. Chances are, the new teacher is just as talented as the previous teacher.

Steinhauser also took full advantage of "skipping" exceptions to the state layoff law that mandates that seniority take precedence during layoffs. Seniority can be ignored if the district demonstrates that certain teachers have specific skills vital to the mission of the school district.[5] For Steinhauser, that meant any teachers trained to teach AP or International Baccalaureate courses. (Nearly 40 percent of Long Beach students are in one program or the other.) "So you could be an AP teacher with three years' experience and not get laid off, and a history teacher with 10 years of service would get laid off." Also exempted were teachers in the district's AVID (Advancement Via Individual Determination) program that is designed to place more "middle performing" students on a college-going track. "That is directly connected to our goal of sending everyone on to a college career," Steinhauser said.

Nearly all the "skipping" decisions involving roughly 150 teachers were approved by an administrative law judge. "Seniority doesn't mean quality versus not quality," Steinhauser said. "Just because you are a new teacher doesn't indicate anything about the quality of your work."

How This Plays Out: Stephens Middle School

Thanks in part to MAP²D, Long Beach educators saw rising math scores in elementary schools, but concluded success in the elementary grades meant little if those same students lost math momentum as they got older. Yet that's exactly what was happening as a result of middle school math teachers not carrying out the same innovations. Making things worse were "gatekeeper" algebra teachers restricting their classes to only high-performing students. In schools such as Stephens Middle, where nearly all the students are minority and come from low-income families, only a trickle ended up in eighth-grade algebra. Steinhauser pushed hard to get more eighth-graders into algebra, a push that wasn't popular with some traditionalist math teachers who feared they would look bad as more of their students failed to score proficient. Their attitude: These students are not prepared! The percentage of my students scoring at the proficient level in algebra will drop! Actually, their fears were understandable. Getting students up to proficiency level is their job.

To make Steinhauser's plan work, middle school math teachers both adopted the successful teaching strategies pioneered in the elementary schools with MAP²D and launched "double dosing" classes: Students could simultaneously take developmental algebra and regular algebra, usually with the same teacher. As always in Long Beach, the new initiative was piloted in the neediest schools, such as Stephens. "We took kids who normally would be in regular seventh- and eighth-grade math, raised the bar, and put them in algebra," said Stephens Principal Diane Prince.

The result? When the initiative started in 2009, less than a third of Stephens students took algebra in the eighth grade. By 2011, 55 percent did. And the widely predicted drop-off in scores never happened: 91 percent of the Stephens students taking algebra scored at the proficient level. Now the program is in all Long Beach middle schools.

Continuous Improvement in Action

A walking tour of Stephens with Prince and math adviser Ed Samuels included a stop at the eighth-grade developmental algebra class taught by Becky Jones, whose teaching garb included a clear plastic apron with scores of markers protruding from the many deep pockets. Clearly, this was a teacher girded for heavy class involvement. "I use more interactive strategies now so they communicate more with each other," Jones said. First the students explain the concept to one another in small groups. Then, a student gets randomly called on to demonstrate before the entire class, a direct spinoff from MAP²D. "They are hearing and seeing it over and over again," she said. "It's not just listening and writing."

The successful track record at Stephens continues despite the layoffs. "Everybody lost teachers," Prince said. "It's horrible. But you know what? We're making it work." Teachers sent in to plug holes proved to be effective from their first day. When the school was short a substitute teacher, a Stephens administrator subbed in. When administrators ran short, the central office loaned out substitute administrators. "You make a phone call to the district and someone shows up," Prince said, "even though you know they should be doing something else."

What makes the difference is Long Beach's long history of focusing on students first, Prince said: "Everybody is here for the kids, even the custodians. We're like a big family. It's just part of our culture. I think part of that comes from our connection through all the training we've received at the district office. It comes from the top down. Everybody values what everybody else is doing."

The Ultimate Test: College Success

Long Beach's success with getting more of its students going to college — nearly 80 percent go on to a two- or four-year college — has played out without an increase in the percentage of its students having to take a remedial college course before enrolling in a for-credit class. "About half our students have to take remedial English," Steinhauser said, "and math is a little higher." Given the expectation that more students going to college means less-qualified students, that has to be considered a positive. But in Long Beach, it's not good enough. To cut that rate, Long Beach launched a pilot with California State University, Long Beach in which students who come up short on a college placement course taken in 11th grade enroll in a 12th-grade English class designed by the university. The seniors who pass that course can automatically enroll in a credit-bearing English class at the university. The same holds true for any student earning a C or better in an AP or International Baccalaureate English class. "We expect to cut in half the number of kids who take remediation," Steinhauser said.

The chemistry of the "Long Beach way" is the secret to its success, according to Steinhauser. The community selected school quality as its top priority, and that became a common culture. Community members run for the school board because they want to reinforce that culture, not because it is a stepping stone to higher office. School board members — and politicians — step aside to let the professionals run the district. "We collaborate," Steinhauser said. "In some cities, you see the mayors either blaming the school system or trying to take over the schools. We don't have that problem here. We have very strong ties with our business community, very strong ties with our community-based organizations. When we revised our social promotion [retention] policy, it went through about a year's process working with teachers, parents, and board members on what it should or should not be. By the time it came to the board to be revised, the teachers presented it to the board, and it was voted on without opposition. We always try to go slow to go fast. We spend a lot of time vetting issues, and, to be honest, we are criticized for that. But we are not flashy. We don't do flavor of the month. We are sort of going on a treadmill that goes from 2.0 to 2.5 to 2.8 and so on. You are not going to see us going from A to Z. It is not going to happen."

Endnotes

1. 2009 data, based on students enrolled within 18 months of high school graduation.

2. Long Beach, Aldine, and Charlotte-Mecklenburg are all winners of the prestigious Broad Prize for Urban Education. Long Beach has reached the finals of the Broad Prize five times.

3. The Fresno-Long Beach Learning Partnership has not been a one-way learning curve. For example, from Fresno, Long Beach learned valuable lessons about structuring summer school: how to identify which students most need summer school and how to use summer school for credit recovery to make more schools eligible for postsecondary study.

4. Many urban school districts resemble departments of public works that just happen to involve schools. In these districts, job preservation takes precedence over student learning.

5. "Skipping" is generally opposed by the unions.

Nancy Grasmick led Maryland public schools to its consistent No. 1 state ranking from Education Week.

Chapter 12

A STATE DESIGNED FOR EXCELLENCE

What's the most reliable way to get Johnny to learn? Every year, put him in a classroom with a great teacher. How do you attract a great teacher? Again, the logic is pretty simple: with a great principal. And what draws a great principal? For starters, it's helpful to have a great district superintendent, and the superintendent will need a supportive school board or mayor or other governance body. But what about state policy? How much does that matter?

By the time you get this far up the ladder from Johnny, the answers get a bit murkier. Because a child's life revolves around the school he attends, we tend to place all the responsibility (and the praise, and the blame) for his experience at the local level. Since the entire nation faces similar achievement gaps and challenges, it's easy to look straight to the federal government for answers. It's easy to discount that bureaucratic rung in the middle.

But does it matter whether Johnny has been to preschool?

Does it matter whether his classroom has a working boiler? Whether his school has a library and enough textbooks in decent shape to go around?

Does it matter if Johnny's teacher knows specifically what to teach him and how to measure his progress?

For all these reasons and more, states play a critical role in their students' learning. *Education Week* has been ranking states for the past 16 years to underscore this point. And for the past four years,

Maryland has come out on top. Maryland has posted greater gains over time than nearly any other state on the National Assessment of Educational Progress (NAEP), dubbed "the nation's report card." It has the highest rate of students earning a passing score on at least one AP Exam, and in 2010, it snagged $250 million in the federal Race to the Top competition. According to *The Washington Post* Challenge Index, Maryland is the state with the highest percentage of rigorous public high schools.

So what sets the Old Line State apart? Once again we must look to see who's standing in front of the class. Maryland had a visionary leader for two decades in Nancy Grasmick, who retired last year as the nation's longest-serving state superintendent. Grasmick put a huge emphasis on early childhood education. She insisted on content standards and established a testing program to hold schools accountable for results years before the No Child Left Behind Act required such a thing. The state has also had several strong district superintendents. Jerry Weast drastically improved results for minority students during his 13 years leading Montgomery County schools, which had the highest graduation rate among the nation's 50 largest systems when he retired in 2011. Bernard Sadusky, Grasmick's interim replacement at the state department, oversaw high performance with an economically diverse population in Queen Anne's County, where he was superintendent from 1994 to 2007.

The other key has been funding. Lawsuits filed in the mid-1990s by the American Civil Liberties Union of Maryland and the city of Baltimore charged the state with denying city students their educational rights. Amid a protracted court battle, the General Assembly passed landmark legislation that poured $1.3 billion into Maryland's 24 school districts between 2003 and 2008. By that point, the state's per-pupil spending had risen by 37 percent in inflation-adjusted dollars since 1990. It hardly seems coincidental that the state started outpacing the nation in its NAEP growth during the same years the increased funding was kicking in.

"In Maryland the gains over time really, really outpace the country," said Baltimore schools chief Andrés Alonso, who sent an email to Grasmick congratulating her when he saw the state's NAEP scores last fall. "We still have the achievement gaps, but what the achievement gaps are masking is that ethnic minorities had double-digit gains. It just so happened that so did the white kids." Of the consistency in the state's successes, Alonso said, "It's evidence of huge focus and a huge investment in education over a stretch of time that's paid off in multiple ways."

That's not to say that Maryland has it all figured out. Alonso presides over what was historically one of the lowest-performing districts in the country, which, while rapidly progressing, still has a long way to go. The state has consistently gotten a B+ as its overall score from *Education Week* — far from perfect, just better than everyone else. The K–12 achievement section of the rankings that explores graduation rates and NAEP scores gave Maryland a B in 2012, compared with a C- for the nation as a whole. As of this publishing, the state school board had yet to name a long-term successor for Grasmick, and many educators and advocates are worried about who will take her place. Loopholes in the state's law requiring local school districts to maintain their contributions to school funding have the potential to undo the years of growth during tough economic times. Maryland schools are struggling with budget cuts and hiring freezes just like everyone else. Even with the state's high school exit exams, too many students still arrive in colleges needing remediation.

Nonetheless, Maryland offers valuable lessons. Let's look deeper.

An Early Investment

Eighteen 4-year-olds in navy pants and white shirts are sitting on an alphabet carpet. Outside on the street around them, many of the houses are boarded up. Here inside their classroom at Tench Tilghman Elementary/Middle School in East Baltimore, they have new cabinets, furniture, and paint. They've been at their lessons since 7:45 a.m., and they'll keep going until 2:45 this afternoon, with only two short breaks in that time for structured play. Now with an hour and a half to go until lunch, a smiling Dorene Creaney asks them to complete her sentences, please.

"A sibling is a ..."

"BROTHER AND A SISTER!"

"We start writing on the ..."

"TOP!"

"And on the ..."

"LEFT!"

"And with a ..."

"CAPITAL LETTER!"

"We have to leave what between our words?"

"SPACE!"

She begins to write on a big white sheet of paper taped to the board:

Siblings stick by each

"I'm out of room," she says when her marker has reached the end of the line, "so I have to come back to the ..."

"LEFT!"

other. Do you have a

sibling?

"I like the way Khalil has his attention up here," says Creaney, a stylish, ponytailed Asian woman in a turquoise scarf, orange sweater, and black pants. "That's how I know he's ..."

"PAYING ATTENTION!"

Maryland has seen a huge return on its investment in prekindergarten programs like this one at Tench Tilghman, where 97 percent of students are African American and 95 percent qualify for free or reduced-price lunches. Two of the children in Creaney's class are homeless, and one has a speech delay. Given that 90 percent of their brain development will have occurred by the time they turn 5, a high-quality preschool program is essential to prevent the cycle of achievement gaps from repeating. Principal Jael Yon was thrilled to have the opportunity a few years ago to use stimulus money to build a prekindergarten wing at her school. Two classes of 23 students (pink eye had hit Creaney's class on the day of our visit) both have a full-time aide assisting the teacher. Thelma Bond, the aide in Creaney's room, has been at the school more than 25 years and instructed not only the children's parents but some of their grandparents as well. She offers an abundance of love and patience.

Maryland's $1.3 billion funding influx sought to level the playing field from the starting line. The aid came with the mandate that schools offer full-day kindergarten for all children and prekindergarten for those whose families are living below 185 percent of the poverty line.

Alongside expansion came quality control. All early childhood programs were transferred to the jurisdiction of the education department, enabling Grasmick's team to tighten the reins on curricula, licensing, professional development, and assessment.

Partnering with community colleges, the state established a scholarship program and other incentives for child care providers to further their studies, and many earned associate degrees. The Maryland Business Roundtable's "Ready At Five" initiative has been instrumental in promoting early learning and communicating best practices. The library system launched a program called "It's Never Too Early" to engage parents and caregivers of young children.

Four out of five children in Maryland now attend some kind of formal early learning center before kindergarten. Forty-three percent are in full-day prekindergarten programs in public schools, which are far more useful to working parents than half-day programs and produce the greatest academic benefits.

The results have been staggering. The state measures the readiness of incoming kindergartners by assessing such skills as speaking clearly, understanding stories, counting, and getting along with others. In the last academic year, 81 percent tested fully ready — up from 49 percent when the Maryland Model for School Readiness began in 2002. The growth among poor and minority children was even more substantial: About three-quarters of both low-income and African American pupils were fully ready for kindergarten versus about a third a decade earlier. What's more, the gains are holding as children age. Those who test fully ready for kindergarten are eight times more likely to earn a proficient score on Maryland's third-grade reading and math exams.

State officials would like to offer prekindergarten to even more families. Guaranteeing admission to those at or below 300 percent of the poverty line would cost an estimated $20 million. Expanding that guarantee to all children would cost $121 million. "It is cost-effectiveness because it's cost-avoidance," Grasmick said. "We are saving so much money in terms of interventions, in terms of dropouts, in terms of low academic performance."

Visionary Leadership

At 73, Nancy Grasmick is supposed to be retired now. But after 20 years at the helm of the Maryland State Department of Education, she just couldn't say no to all the invitations to serve on boards and commissions that flooded in upon her departure in 2011. Nor could she resist the urge to tackle a problem that she didn't feel she had the power to address all these years: teacher preparation. When this book went to press, she was weighing her job options in that arena.

Grasmick, who is married to the wealthy owner of a lumber company and began her career teaching deaf students in Baltimore, never had any children biologically. During her run as the nation's longest-serving state superintendent, she was fond of saying she was the mother of 850,000. Poised and charming, she proved herself to be brilliant at navigating tumultuous political waters as she advocated tirelessly for her education agenda.

In the late 1980s, a state commission chaired by the late Walter Sondheim — a legend in Baltimore civic life who led the charge for desegregation as chair of the city school board in the 1950s — called for the establishment of an accountability system: Set standards for student learning, test the students on them, and measure the schools' progress accordingly. It was a radical idea for a state at the time, a full decade before No Child Left Behind. Grasmick, appointed in 1991, embraced the concept.

Three years later, she rolled out the Maryland School Performance Assessment Program for third-, fifth-, and eighth-graders. It was in many ways a dream test: It did not contain a single multiple-choice item. Nor was it divided into subject areas. Students might be graded on their grammar for one question and on science content for the next. "They drew graphs, they wrote, they explained, they interpreted," said Leslie Wilson, assistant state superintendent of testing and accountability. "They planted seeds on Monday and watched them sprout through the week. Butterfly cocoons hatched. It was really very engaging for the students. For those scoring it, it was a little bit tough."

With the advent of NCLB, the test was no longer viable — first, because it wasn't administered to every grade, and second, because it resulted in scores for schools but not for individual students. The largely multiple-choice tests that replaced it were more rudimentary. They did, however, break ground in another area: They measured student mastery of a uniform state curriculum, which a Grasmick-appointed panel deemed necessary and developed over several years in a process involving thousands of teachers. "You know how independent different districts are, but they all said, 'Yes, we love it, we want it,'" recalled Mary Cary, assistant state superintendent of instruction.

Travana Eades was thrilled when her school recommended she take an AP class.

The so-called Voluntary State Curriculum became the subject of a running joke, Cary said: "How could it be voluntary if all the assessments were based on it?"

No Child Left Behind came into being just as the curriculum was being formed and the massive funding infusion was about to take effect. Serendipitous timing. "There were a lot of states that were outraged because they didn't have anything," Grasmick said. "We had an accountability system, and we were going to have a statewide curriculum, so we didn't see the transition as being that staggering. For us the transition was really minimal."

There was also the matter of high school graduation standards. Grasmick felt passionately that a Maryland high school diploma needed to mean something. She pushed for new state graduation exams, which replaced earlier tests so easy that most students could pass them in sixth grade and many districts made them a requirement to enter high school, not leave it. After years of debate, the new exams in English, algebra, biology, and government became graduation requirements in 2009.[1] The widespread fears that large numbers of students would be denied diplomas have not materialized, but several students — 8 percent, or 5,012 graduates in the class of 2011 — have needed to exercise their right to do project alternatives.

Grasmick saw the graduation exams as measuring a floor, not a ceiling. That's why she was such a strong proponent of the Advanced Placement Program.

Setting the Bar High

When a boy with chronic disciplinary issues kept landing in Gina Davenport's office complaining that his classes were too boring, she devised an unlikely consequence: She enrolled him in an AP class. By the end of the school year, the same child who failed ninth-grade English had passed an AP Exam, earning him college credit. Sufficiently challenged, his behavior problems went away.

Davenport is the assistant principal at Arundel High, a school of nearly 2,000 students located 15 miles northwest of Annapolis in a flat, leafy suburb. Arundel's enrollment is 60 percent white and 40 percent minority. Many students are first-generation Americans, and the population is transient because of its proximity to the Fort Meade Army base.

Arundel is one of many high schools in Maryland that have heeded the state's call for increased course rigor. Since opening admission to AP classes, the school nearly tripled its participation and doubled its pass rate on AP Exams. In 2006, Arundel students took 459 AP Exams and earned 311 passing scores. By 2011, the number of exams had jumped to 1,226, of which 663 were passing. "We can create an AP student out of any student with the right supports," said Davenport, a kindly and no-nonsense woman who annually finds herself loaning her personal money to kids for exam fees. The question Arundel counselors pose to any student expressing interest in college is not, "Do you want to take an AP class?" but rather, "Which AP class will you take?"

Maryland works in close partnership with the College Board to ensure broad and equitable access to AP courses. The College Board has a full-time liaison who works out of the Maryland State Department of Education writing grants to support AP expansion in schools with high-poverty populations, and it provides ongoing professional development to teachers, administrators, and school counselors.

For three straight years, Maryland had the nation's highest percentage of seniors earning at least one passing score on an AP Exam. The state also ranked first in the percentage of seniors taking AP Exams in math and science. It was second to Florida in the total number of seniors completing an AP Exam: 43.4 percent, versus Florida's 43.5 percent. It was in the top five states for its pass rate among African American students, and it eliminated the achievement gap for Hispanics, who make up 7.1 percent of the population and accounted for 7.7 percent of the seniors passing AP Exams.

Arundel offers AP courses in 26 subjects, from Music Theory to Calculus BC. "You can really take an AP class in every subject except gym," said 17-year-old Drew Danick, a tall, skinny blonde kid who will be the first in his family to go to college. Naturally smart, he "pretty much never" had to study before he started taking AP classes. When we visited, he was pushing himself to understand vector multiplication in AP Physics C.

The school has a daily "Wildcat Hour," where everyone goes to lunch at the same time so students have access to all their teachers for extra help. On several "Super Saturdays" leading up to AP Exams, a half-dozen teachers or more volunteer to do study sessions. The honor society provides peer tutoring, and a program that seeks to level the playing field for low-income and minority students also offers support. One of the nine sections of AP Human Geography has a special education teacher working alongside the regular teacher to make the course accessible to a handful of students with learning disabilities. Among them is Dionte Cain, 18, who surprised both his mother and his school counselor when he informed them that he wanted to take an AP class based on a friend's suggestion. He'd spent most of his high school career until that point getting in trouble but decided he was ready to change. "Of course it started out rough, but I'm getting used to it," he said in November. "It's like having two classes in one. They give me as much help as any student needs, but it all comes down to me." He wants to go to culinary school and manage a restaurant.

With a stable teaching force and administration and high parental involvement, a school like Arundel was ripe to flourish under the right state and district policies. Moving the needle was and remains far harder in what was long one of the nation's lowest-performing school districts: Baltimore.

All Hands on Deck

Even as Maryland has established a reputation for itself as an academic powerhouse, many people still associate Baltimore schools with the HBO series *The Wire*. And the series' portrayal of a system mired in cronyism, incompetence, and bureaucracy was accurate for a long time. As the highly politicized city school system went through one chief executive officer after another under a structure of mayoral control, it didn't seem to matter much what the state did. In exchange for a funding infusion, the state gained partial oversight in 1997 through the creation of a new school board jointly appointed by the mayor and the governor. Performance began to nudge up very slowly, but the partnership was not amicable. Animosity climaxed in 2006, when Grasmick tried to take over 11 failing middle and high schools, and the General Assembly voted to block her amid bitter local resistance.

Things began to change in 2007 with the school board's appointment of Andrés Alonso, a Cuban immigrant with four Ivy League degrees and little patience for excuses. Alonso slashed the bloated central office to divert more resources to schools, closed failing schools (including most of those Grasmick had targeted), and opened innovative new ones. He sent staff to bang on the doors of kids who weren't showing up to school. The central tenet of his reform has been establishing accountability on each rung of the ladder down to Johnny. Yes, the state's rung matters — a lot — but so do all the other steps below.

Alonso gave principals autonomy in exchange for results; today, only about a quarter of the principals there in 2007 are still at their jobs. His administration negotiated a new contract tying teacher pay to performance evaluations and giving teachers voting power to change their own working conditions, such as the length of the school day. "He embraced the city–state partnership and was more than willing to use the expertise of the state," Grasmick said. "We did have a really strong relationship. We met every two weeks; we spent hours discussing issues."

While Baltimore schools are still nowhere near where they need to be in terms of test scores, their dropout rate is at its lowest in decades. Enrollment is up for the first time in 40 years, partly due to the continued expansion of prekindergarten, which went from 3,050 seats in 2006 to 4,840 last year. The system got out from under a special education lawsuit that drained money and resources for more than a quarter-century. Federal officials announced the results of the 2011 Trial Urban District Assessment — NAEP scores broken down to compare urban systems — in Baltimore as acknowledgment of city students' progress in math. "This is a work in progress, Baltimore," Grasmick said.

In 2004, Baltimore high schools offered 44 AP courses. Last year they offered 138. Participation went from 823 to 2,669 during that time. As the city replaced a zoned high school assignment process with student choice and redistributed funds according to enrollment, many high schools added AP courses to give themselves a competitive advantage: It looks bad if the principal at the high school fair booth next to yours offers AP and you don't.

So access was the first step. Next is getting more students to pass the tests. Baltimore students had 500 passing scores on AP Exams last year, up from 290 the year Alonso arrived but "still a really lousy pass rate," he acknowledged. A massive professional development effort is under way. Middle schools are introducing honors courses and dramatically expanding eighth-grade algebra to prepare students for high school rigor. Eight high schools new to AP are taking advantage of the state's partnership offers and working closely with the College Board liaison.

One such school is Vivien T. Thomas Medical Arts Academy, created in the breakup of a big failing high school in the city's bleak southwestern corner. Walking through the halls, Principal Starletta Jackson's expectations for her 500 students are clear. The uniform is a medical lab coat. Misbehaving results in mopping duty, and the floors are gleaming. ("Cleanliness is next to godliness," Jackson says.) The walls are filled with photos of African Americans successful in the medical field, from Daniel Hale Williams, who performed the first successful open-heart surgery, to Mary Eliza Mahoney, the first African American registered nurse in the United States.

Standardized test scores at Vivien T. Thomas generally don't indicate that students are ready for AP, but Jackson has introduced five subjects anyway and is utilizing the available resources at every rung of the ladder to pull her students up. They are, in turn, trying to climb. Juniors formed the Motivation Club to support each other in the rigorous courses. Sophomore Travana Eades, 15, said her family was so excited when she was recommended to take AP U.S. Government and Politics that "my mother went and told the whole church."

"I didn't realize I was capable," Travana said. "It brings out the best in me."

Endnotes

1. The government test has since been eliminated because of budget cuts, and all the assessments will be revamped in 2014-15 to align with a revised state curriculum linked with recently adopted common national standards.

Eduardo Padrón's office is in a building adorned with flags representing the many home countries of Miami Dade College students.

Chapter 13

REWORKING REMEDIATION

On July 21, 1961, a boy said good-bye to his parents, not knowing if he would ever see them again. They were sending him, at 15, with his brother, 12, to America to escape Fidel Castro's oppressive regime in their native Cuba. His mother, who had only completed third grade, made him promise her that he would go to college someday. She said it would be his passport to everything.

In Miami, the boy, Eduardo José Padrón, found himself in a beautiful Mediterranean Revival–style tower that at one time housed *The Miami News* and had been converted into a center for the U.S. government to process Cuban refugees. He thought he and his brother were headed for an orphanage, but a woman who knew his parents recognized them and took them in. For a year and a half, he struggled through high school while working three or four jobs at a time, then spent the few dollars he had saved on college application fees. He was rejected everywhere except the one place anyone could go: the local community college.[1]

Fast-forward to Dec. 2, 2010. Padrón, now the president of Miami Dade College (the word "community" was dropped when he introduced the first bachelor's degree programs in 2003), is hosting a fundraiser in the old refugee processing center, now property of the college and listed on the National Register of Historic Places as the Freedom Tower.[2] The crowd of 700 is a who's who of Miami, from political and civic figures to Gloria and Emilio Estefan. In a single night, Padrón raises $5 million to establish the American

Dream Scholarship Fund, guaranteeing any senior in Miami public high schools with a B average or better a two-year college education regardless of financial circumstances.

Under Padrón's leadership since 1995, Miami Dade College has 174,000 students on eight campuses, making it the largest college in the United States. It enrolls more Hispanics and graduates more black and Hispanic students with associate degrees than any other American institution of higher education. Ninety percent of its students are minorities, and 67 percent are low income; they represent 185 countries and speak 91 languages.[3] Padrón has built the college into an iconic cultural institution, one that draws 400,000 attendees each November at a weeklong book fair and showcases more than 100 films from 35 countries at the annual Miami International Film Festival. It makes sculpture gardens, art galleries, and the latest technology accessible to the poorest residents of the nation's third-poorest city. "Democracy's College," Padrón likes to call it.

Danyelle Carter, a 24-year-old studying business management, says her community perceives the college "almost like a hero." She didn't think college was for her until she saw a Miami Dade commercial on television featuring students she could relate to talking about their experiences. Her enrollment inspired four of her relatives — her mother, brother, sister, and sister-in-law — to follow suit; they are all scheduled to graduate together this spring, Danyelle with a bachelor's and the others with associate degrees.

Each of the last three sitting U.S. presidents has visited Miami Dade College. Barack Obama was last year's commencement speaker. When the Republican presidential candidates went stomping through Florida in January, Mitt Romney held a public forum with the Spanish language channel Univisión in a Miami Dade College auditorium, and Newt Gingrich had Padrón escort him to a taping at the nearby Univisión studio. Both sides of the political aisle recognize the college as a place that is making an enormous social and economic impact, producing Miami's teachers, its firefighters, its cops, its nurses, its insurance adjusters. Five years after completing their degrees, graduates in the class of 2005 earned an average of $63,016 in 2010 versus $45,684 for the average worker in the regional labor market that year.

To get results like that, Miami Dade College is tackling what is perhaps this country's greatest educational struggle: students showing up to college unprepared for college-level work. Throughout the book, we've told stories of extraordinary people and institutions preparing students for college. But then the question becomes, what happens when they get there? Nationally, the reality is grim. The majority of students enrolling in community colleges need to take at least one remedial course, and only a quarter of students in remedial courses earn a degree within eight years, according to the Bill & Melinda Gates Foundation, which is investing up to $110 million to address the issue. Remedial education is costing this country an estimated $2 billion a year, and its challenges extend to four-year institutions. A quarter of bachelor's degree students need remediation, too.

While Miami Dade College by no means has the problem solved, it is retaining students at significantly higher rates than peer institutions, despite the fact that more of them need remediation. Nationally, 60 percent of students require at least one remedial course. At Miami Dade, 74 percent do. Yet at Miami Dade, 71 percent of degree-seeking students return for a second year, compared with 56 percent in a 2009 national study of community colleges.[4] Nearly two-thirds of Miami Dade graduates began in remedial courses. "We're dealing with the most difficult, challenging population you could ever imagine in terms of income, in terms of language, in terms of level of preparedness for college, etc., etc. And yet the achievement of our students is significant," said Padrón, the kind of man who appears far taller than he actually is. He has a shaved head and a neat mustache and wears thin glasses and well-tailored suits. His commanding presence and passion, rooted in his humble beginnings, have galvanized an institution around the vision that everyone can rise to greatness.

The Remediation Crisis

An all-too-common scenario goes something like this: Armed with a high school diploma, a kid shows up to begin community college. He takes a placement test only to discover that he doesn't have the reading, writing, and math skills required to do college-level work. He must invest time and money into taking remedial courses that will not earn him any credit. He grows discouraged and disillusioned — wasn't his high school diploma supposed to mean something? — and drops out. Studies have found that many students graduating high school with a 3.0 GPA or better still wind up in remediation.

Scenario B, all too common as well: A high school graduate goes straight into the workforce. After some years of menial, low-paying jobs, she decides to go back to school. She might appreciate the refresher that remedial courses offer, but the time and energy required before she can even start earning credit are too much as she struggles to take classes while working and supporting a family.[5] She has to run a race just to get to the starting line.

With the prohibitive cost of four-year schools, more than seven million students are pursuing degrees at 1,200 community colleges in the United States, representing nearly half of all those enrolled in college.[6] Community colleges are, for so many low-income, minority students, the only affordable option to make the dream of higher education achievable. They are the centerpiece of Obama's American Graduation Initiative to restore the country to having the highest proportion of college graduates in the world by 2020. We are highlighting community colleges here rather than four-year colleges because they offer the best insight into the issues confronting so many of the students targeted in this book.

Graduation rates at many community colleges are dismal as students languish in remedial classes, and tough budgetary times are stalling numerous reforms. But innovation is emerging nevertheless. The City University of New York, for example, is opening a new community college this summer that will scrap remedial courses entirely, with the idea that everyone will come in needing some degree of skill reinforcement. Students will be required to enroll full time and take a core set of classes their first year, getting extensive support while earning credit. West Kentucky Community & Technical College has improved retention by training faculty to address students' poor reading skills in all subjects, not just remedial courses. Padrón is impressed with systemic reforms in Virginia's community colleges to give students only the units of math remediation they need, rather than requiring them to sit through entire courses that repeat some material they already know.

The Aspen Institute is spending $1 million a year to reward and draw attention to places with practices worth replicating. The $600,000 Aspen Prize for Community College Excellence went last year to Valencia College in Orlando, Fla., where more than half of students graduate or transfer within three years, compared with fewer than 40 percent nationally. (Selected from a pool of 1,000 applicants, Miami Dade was one of four "finalists with distinction" receiving $100,000; West Kentucky was another.) With data showing that students' experiences in their first five college courses determine their eventual success, Valencia overhauled its admissions, advising, and orientation processes to provide more information and support at the onset. It was willing to risk state funding by prohibiting students from enrolling in classes after the first day. Latecomers are less likely to complete a course, but with funding based on enrollment, community colleges have a perverse incentive to enroll as many students as possible even if they are setting them up for failure. Valencia solved this problem by creating a second set of course offerings with a later start date, maintaining its accessibility and funding while raising expectations.

The Gates Foundation work is allowing colleges such as Miami Dade to design and implement strategies to keep students motivated as they catch up academically. At a 2010 convention, Melinda Gates told community college leaders that they can keep doing what they've been doing — and meet the needs of fewer and fewer students — or they can innovate. "You can educate your students according to new models that yield dramatically better results for a fraction of the cost," she said.

For a glimpse into some of those new models, we travel to Miami Dade College.

Intervention Individualized

It's Tuesday afternoon in downtown Miami, and 30 students in a fluorescent-lit classroom are solving linear equations with one variable. The college offers three levels of remedial math; this is the middle one.

If F divided by 2 minus 5 equals 1, then F divided by 2 equals 6.

The teacher, Redelcarmen Sarduy, who has chin-length hair dyed dark red, black high heels, and caring eyes, asks if they understand.

"Explain it one more time," a young man says.

"No, don't explain it one more time. Dude, if you don't get it by now ..." says a girl in a plaid shirt, arms crossed.

Sarduy explains anyway, and they multiply both sides by 2 to solve F as 12. "Perfect!" she exclaims often.

Similar scenes play out in community college classrooms around the country, but Sarduy's students have several things going for them that others in remedial education do not. There are the tangible reforms: a comprehensive effort at the college to improve math instruction, Sarduy's availability along with other faculty and peer mentors at a tutoring center, and the life skills students are learning in another course. But something intangible is going on as well. Collectively, the college's initiatives and programs create a whole that is bigger than the sum of its parts, an environment of no excuses and a culture of success.

Everyone in need of remediation at Miami Dade is required to simultaneously take a credit-bearing course called Student Life Skills. SLS, as it's called, covers the gamut of topics from types of learning styles to time management to résumé writing to goal setting. It covers the importance of persisting when things get tough, of assuming accountability for a problem even when it isn't your fault. Each student must develop a personalized plan setting a path to graduation with a particular major. The plan outlines which courses to take and when, and what resources the college has to help. Miami Dade offers different versions of SLS depending on students' needs, and the course has been found to nearly double the graduation rate among the students with the greatest academic deficiencies.

"In my class, students get to understand themselves," said Jocelyne Legrand, who has been teaching the life skills course at Miami Dade for the past 22 years and working at the college for 30, since she was a young Haitian immigrant. She is one of many who, like Padrón, come to the college and end up staying for life.[7] One of Legrand's favorite assignments is asking students to make a collage of images showing what they want their lives to look like. She varies her class discussion topics based on students' challenges, whether with financial aid, difficulty in a relationship with a professor, transportation, or deciding on a major. "They know that this is a place to look for answers to questions," she said. "It gives them a chance to succeed."

The college has been getting more sophisticated in its scheduling. Students may now take credit-bearing and remedial courses alongside one another instead of having to take all their remedial courses first. A student who needs extra help in math might still be able to take a credit-bearing history course. One whose English needs brushing up might still be able to succeed in college-level math. For the many students learning English as a second language, the college is beginning to incorporate reading into specific programs of study. In math, it is turning a combination of remedial math and statistics into a yearlong, credit-bearing course. Two of the college's campuses are piloting a mentoring program that electronically pairs students with faculty members and alumni, giving them more communication options than traditional mentor programs have.

A sense of possibility is palpable touring Miami Dade's North Campus, where the administration has done an extraordinary job leveraging the power of grants and donations amid state budget cuts to create a 245-acre oasis in a very poor neighborhood. Artists have donated close to 70 sculptures to form a sculpture park. Pick up a headset in the library, and you can take a guided 1.5-mile tour like you're in a museum. A "Palmetum" includes every species of palm tree that exists in the world, 400 of them. A computer courtyard has 500 stations where students can write papers and access the Internet. A new $40 million science building so impressed University of Florida officials that they established a microbiology program enabling Miami Dade students to continue for a bachelor's degree under the same roof while the university accesses superior lab equipment. Campus President José Vicente is not joking when he says he wants to see Florida rival California and New York as an entertainment capital, starting with his new surround-sound cinema, video screening room, and sound recording studio to prepare students for jobs in the field. On the day we visited, singer Jon Secada was guest teaching. "State of the art" was the phrase Vicente used most often on the tour.

With a science and technology–themed preschool to give early childhood education majors hands-on experience and a program training morticians, the North Campus serves its community from cradle to grave. It makes a deliberate effort to host events for children and young teens so they and their families will feel comfortable on a college campus. More than 4,000 Miami public school students participated in a citywide science fair held there earlier this year. One Saturday each December, the campus converts itself into a "Christmas wonderland" where last year 35,000 people came for pony rides, a parade, and Santa Claus landing in a helicopter.

An almost missionary zeal extends throughout the college. Miami Dade was Florida's first racially integrated community college, and it has long been known for its extensive services to newly arrived immigrants and refugees. Poor families can go for free to six art galleries and three public art spaces and see works by the likes of Francisco de Goya y Lucientes. They can attend community theater productions in Spanish and take acting and creative writing classes. Literacy campaigns distribute thousands of free books and target first- and second-graders. The "Miami: City of Refuge" program provides a safe haven for writers persecuted in their countries and forced into exile. Michelle Obama presented service learning awards at the Freedom Tower a few years back; during the 2010-11 academic year, 7,193 students tallied 163,720 hours of community service.

"It's very unique in this country," said Padrón, who has been named one of the 10 best college presidents by *Time* magazine, Floridian of the Year by *Florida Trend* magazine, and one of the eight most influential college presidents by *The Washington Post*. "You have places like Harvard, Yale, but most of their graduates do not stay there. They come from different places and leave when they graduate. The people we graduate in Miami Dade, most of them stay here, so Miami Dade is like an icon that is greatly supported and greatly respected."

Taking Stock Early

Responsibility. It is human nature to pass off what isn't yours. A college's job is to educate students in college, not students in high school. A high school's job is to educate high school students, not those in middle school. But solving the nation's crisis in remedial education is going to require a collective sense of responsibility beyond any assigned titles or roles. "The boundaries we create between K–12 and higher education make it difficult for colleges to figure out how to use their resources to help more students arrive prepared," said Joshua Wyner, executive director of Aspen's College Excellence Program, which administers the Aspen Prize. If a college works with its local high schools to reduce the number of students arriving in need of remediation, "the state will not reimburse you for that work," Wyner said. "You have to be committed to student success above all else." And that's exactly what's happening in Miami.

Take Tom Albano, executive director of Miami Dade's office of precollege programs. A native New Yorker whose own two children are enrolled at the college, Albano runs a variety of programs to ensure that kids in Miami both graduate from high school and arrive in college ready for college-level work. The students in those programs could go anywhere, but the reality is that 7 in 10 public high school graduates in Miami who attend college in Florida attend Miami Dade. Assuming responsibility for them before they arrive isn't just the right thing to do. It's common sense.

One of the programs under Albano's watch is called Take Stock in Children, which since 1995 has existed as a high school completion program in school districts around Florida. Miami Dade is also looking at it to curb remediation rates by giving students an incentive to stay engaged academically through their senior year of high school. Low-income students are selected in middle school to sign a contract where they and their parents commit that they will maintain at least a 2.0 GPA and stay drug and crime free. In exchange, the college gives each student a mentor, monthly college-prep workshops — and a college scholarship that covers tuition at Miami Dade or can be applied anywhere. Call it the carrot-and-stick approach. "It was so, so inspirational and motivating," said Adrian Lima, 19, who graduated from high school last year and is now attending Miami Dade's prestigious Honors College as a civil engineering major.

Of the 550 students participating in Take Stock Miami, four have lost scholarships for breaking the contract. Last year, 100 percent of the high school seniors in the program graduated, and 100 percent enrolled in college. Statewide, Take Stock participants graduate college at a rate 25 percent higher than Florida's average and 140 percent higher than their at-risk peer group. Not only are students showing up to college, they're coming more prepared, and they're staying there. "This is a program that works," Albano said. "This is a program that should go nationwide."

An intention for collaboration was behind recent Florida legislation requiring students to take the state's college placement exam in 11th grade and spend their senior year doing whatever remediation is needed to graduate college ready. As of this publication, however, the mandate remained unfunded and was not happening. Miami Dade and Florida International University administrators were still working with local high schools for the coming academic year to bring remedial college curricula to struggling seniors.

Padrón has an even more radical idea. He'd like to eliminate the senior year of high school, which he says is "really a wasted year" during which students forget valuable skills when they aren't sufficiently challenged. Instead, he would have college-ready students start earning credit with dual enrollment in college courses. Those who need remediation could do it then. Padrón recognizes that the idea isn't particularly viable politically but says it would "save a lot of lives."

Are so many students in need of remediation because elementary and secondary schools aren't teaching basic skills? Or is the issue that students aren't retaining what they've learned? It seems to be a combination of the two. Retention is a huge problem, as evidenced by the fact that students who wait more than a year after high school before enrolling at Miami Dade are much more likely to need remediation: 91 percent in 2010. Madeline Pumariega, president of Miami Dade's Wolfson Campus downtown, said her view of the situation changed a few years ago when her 7-year-old daughter was in kindergarten. The little girl would get a dozen vocabulary words each Monday to memorize for a quiz each Friday. Every week she'd get 100 on the quiz, only to have forgotten the words two weeks later when the teacher didn't reinforce them. The experience illustrated to Pumariega the importance of keeping students engaged in material after an exam is done, and the limitations of basing high-stakes decisions on a single test score. The American public education system revolves around students passing tests, but then what? The question is one that Miami Dade plans to address with its Gates funding. For all the college's accomplishments, Pumariega said, "the mission is never complete. We need to graduate more students and do it more effectively."

Inclusion and Excellence

When Eduardo Padrón got to what was then called Dade County Junior College, his only aspiration was what he considered the American Dream: to be rich. So he studied economics. After receiving his associate degree, he went on to earn a bachelor's from Florida Atlantic University and master's and doctoral degrees from the University of Florida. (During those years, his parents finally made it over from Cuba, and the family happily reunited.) Interviewing for jobs around the country was Padrón's first chance to see the United States beyond Florida. He accepted a position with DuPont in Wilmington, Del., then went back to the junior college to tell his old professors the great news. To his surprise, they gave him a guilt trip about going to work for a "corporate monster." He decided to stay and teach economics there for a year, and then he would go out and make money. The rest, as they say, is history.

Padrón approaches his work with the eye of an economist. As an administrator at the Wolfson Campus in the 1980s, he started "Books by the Bay" with 14 tables of reading material to draw people to Miami's struggling downtown. The Miami International Book Fair is now the largest literary event in the United States. Miami Dade College contributes an estimated $4 billion annually to the county's economy through student productivity, college operations, and student spending. Many community colleges are focused on equipping students with specific job skills, but Miami Dade is particularly adept at creating career pipelines to fuel the local workforce. This is significant for retention because studies show that students are more likely to keep going if they are clear about their major and have a clear career path. And associate degree recipients at Miami Dade are gaining a competitive advantage in the job market over their peers from four-year institutions. *The Miami Herald* reported last year that bachelor's degree recipients from Florida's 11 public universities earned an average starting salary of $36,552 in 2009, compared with $47,708 for associate degree recipients from community colleges.

Padrón is only the college's fourth president since its founding in 1960. At all five of the community colleges the Aspen Institute recognized last year, the presidents have been in their positions for more than a decade, providing as Padrón does stability but not complacency. Aspen's Wyner said they have created a sense of urgency that the status quo is not good enough and then empowered faculty to make changes. Padrón is a self-described perfectionist who is incredibly demanding, while giving his staff the freedom to take their ideas and run with them. He is as comfortable mingling with the world's power brokers as he is with his students and their families. A "Presidential Moments" section in a recent college publication shows photos of him smiling with the likes of Jill Biden, Shakira, and Queen Sofia of Spain. "Whenever he walks into the room, he's just so friendly and kind, and I start getting nervous because he inspires me to be someone great," said Kathryn Sotolongo, 19, a mass communications major in the Honors College who is active in student government.

On the day Padrón hosted Mitt Romney in January, he was fighting a cough that had kept him awake the previous two nights. Waiting for Romney's tour bus to arrive, he slipped into a bathroom to wash his hands so as not to spread germs with his many handshakes and alternately replied to emails on his phone and chatted with a local reporter and Javier Palomarez, president of the U.S. Hispanic Chamber of Commerce. When the bus pulled up, he greeted the candidate and his wife and eased into conversation despite the surrounding security and gaggle of photographers. Romney wanted to know if the college has dorms. No, Padrón replied, everyone commutes.

Padrón relies on high-powered connections to keep the college thriving amid major challenges to its state funding. The state's contribution to the college's $343 million operating budget has been steadily declining, leaving many departments short-staffed, and as this book was going to press, Florida's public colleges and universities were bracing for even steeper cuts. A recent report by the National Education Association ranked Florida 46th among the states for its level of instructional staff at public colleges and universities and 49th for noninstructional staff. Miami Dade Provost Rolando Montoya said that the college's 2,317 full-time staff members do the work of about 3,000.[8] Padrón sets the example, working around the clock. Grants and private fundraising enable Miami Dade to keep building and running special programs. Last year, the college was awarded $33 million in grants and raised $10.6 million in donations. Perhaps the most meaningful in-kind donation for Padrón was the Freedom Tower, which had gone into private hands and was donated to the college by developers in 2005. It is now a cultural arts center.

Connections have also enabled Miami Dade to assemble advisory councils of high-powered professionals in various fields, keeping its 300 degree programs current, and to form a massive roster of partnerships. The New World School of the Arts is a combined high school and bachelor's degree program for artistically gifted students run in collaboration with the K–12 system and the University of Florida. High school students are admitted solely on the basis of artistic talent, but they post some of the highest standardized test scores in the state. The college's new Miami Culinary Institute is the one affordable culinary school in the area, and it is establishing itself as a leader in the farm-to-table movement, focusing on good nutrition and environmentally sustainable practices in a gleaming LEED-certified building. Frank Nero, president of the Beacon Council, Miami's official economic development partnership, said Padrón has broken the stereotype that community college programs must be second rate. "What he does, he does first class," Nero said. "That's a good lesson for many community colleges: You don't have to play second fiddle." In other places, power brokers might not want to advertise their associate degrees, but among the politicians, CEOs, journalists, and others who got their start at Miami Dade College, they are almost like a badge of honor.

"The one thing I have learned, and I think we have demonstrated here, is that inclusion and excellence can go hand in hand," Padrón said. "The American university model is one of exclusion. You select the students who you want to work with, and you keep out the rest. Many of my colleagues take pride in how many students applied who they didn't admit. We take pride in admitting everybody with a high school diploma and making something out of them. I think that's the secret. It's not easy. It's not cheap. But it's what America needs more of, to harness the potential of every human being."

Endnotes

1. The college has gone through three names. Established in 1960 as Dade County Junior College, it was renamed Miami-Dade Community College in 1973 and Miami Dade College (dropping the hyphen in Miami-Dade) in 2003.

2. In the fall of 2011, the college enrolled 2,541 students in baccalaureate programs.

3. The college's diversity extends to its staff: Three-quarters of full-time employees are minorities.

4. Last year, the college enrolled 96,036 credit-bearing and 70,806 non-credit-bearing students. The remainder of the 174,000 enrolled for short-term courses and workshops.

5. Sixty-nine percent of Miami Dade students work, and 20 percent work full time. Sixty-one percent attend the college part time. The average student age is 26.

6. American community colleges enroll 13 million students total; among them, about seven million are seeking degrees.

7. Forty-one percent of full-time faculty and 30 percent of all full-time employees have been at the college more than 15 years.

8. The college also has 4,034 part-time employees.

Conclusion

IF THE DREAM IS ACHIEVABLE, WE MUST ACT

Equity, it turns out, was on the minds of a lot of voters during the 2012 Republican presidential primaries. Just two days after the New Hampshire primary, the Pew Research Center released a poll showing that two-thirds of Americans believed there were "strong conflicts" between rich and poor, a 50 percent rise since 2009, when the pollsters last asked that question. "Income inequality is no longer just for economists," said Richard Morin, a senior editor at Pew Social & Demographic Trends. "It has moved off the business pages into the front page."[1] Not that "equity" means the same thing to all voters. For the moment, set aside the polar opposites, Occupy Wall Street and the Tea Party, and focus on the broad middle. To Democrats, "equity" means tapping the brakes on the rich-getting-richer phenomenon. To Republicans, it means shrinking government to preserve individual freedoms. But nearly everyone, even the most doctrinaire of the Tea Party, agrees with the importance of preserving the essential foundation of "Americanism": Everyone deserves equity of opportunity.

That brings the debate directly to the schoolhouse door. What other institution in the United States is held accountable for providing equity of opportunity? And when more people learn that education equity is possible, as we did while researching this book, they will reach the same conclusion we have reached: If the dream is achievable, then we must act to achieve it. Taking no action toward achieving equity is the costliest of options.

Students who fail to earn high school diplomas, for example, cost this country billions.[2]

Few would argue, however, that the American education system provides that equity, not when 60 percent of community college students (in some states, as many as 80 percent) and a fifth of students entering bachelor's degree programs have to take at least one remedial course before becoming eligible to take credit-bearing courses.[3] State University of New York Chancellor Nancy Zimpher estimates that remedial education costs that state $70 million a year, more than the budget for eight entire SUNY campuses.[4]

Preparing students for college or job training programs is the fundamental responsibility handed to school districts. Are they succeeding?

Not when less than 50 percent of black males in many cities even make it through high school: How many high school dropouts have a shot at a decent job?

Not when many high schools restrict access to their college-pipeline courses: How can students prepare for college if they don't take college-preparation classes?

Not when the highest-performing teachers always end up in schools in the highest-income neighborhoods: In Los Angeles schools, poor and minority children are twice as likely to draw low-rated teachers.[5] Hasn't the research proven that having high-quality teachers is paramount?

Not when some school districts, especially urban districts where students most need the help, organize themselves in ways that favor teachers and administrators over students. Why are so many low-performing school districts unable to fire their worst teachers so that more effective teachers can take over?

The bottom line: Latino and African American high school seniors turn in math and reading scores that mirror those of 13-year-old white students. "We take kids that start [high school] a little behind and by the time they finish high school, they're way behind," said Amy Wilkins from The Education Trust, a Washington-based group that advocates for poor and minority students. "That's the opposite of what American values say education is about. Education is supposed to level the playing field, and it does the opposite."[6]

There is a way out of this unfair system, a way to achieve the dream. That's why we wrote this book, to share lessons learned.

First and foremost: Boost teacher quality, step up the academic rigor of courses, and spread those more rigorous courses to more students. Simply measured, rigor is the knowledge students need to succeed beyond high school, either in job training programs or college. How will we know if the strategy is working? Not just by grades, not only by passing scores on AP Exams or the number of International Baccalaureate diplomas earned. Rather, we will know the system is moving toward equity when the college remediation rates decline. The surest sign of a lack of rigor in the K–12 grades is the extraordinary number of students forced to take noncredit courses, especially in community colleges, to learn what should have been learned in high school. In many cases, high schools may be trying to present rigorous course work, but they aren't doing it in such a way that students actually retain information. This is why we must dive deep into the art and, yes, the science of effective instruction — even as early as preschool.

In today's economy, the only way to earn wages that are livable — and hopefully better than livable — is through higher education. Eighty percent of the fastest-growing jobs require some kind of postsecondary study. But we'll never achieve equity of opportunity without whittling down the college remediation rates. Students who come from families with limited means and almost no college-going traditions can't afford to pay thousands of dollars in tuition to take noncredit courses to make up for where their high schools failed them. No wonder fewer of them end up earning degrees.[7]

We know, we are making it sound so simple. What school isn't trying to boost teacher quality, step up academic rigor, and engage more students in tough course work? But trying and succeeding are worlds apart. Often what looks like progress, or even success, in elementary, middle, or high school gets deflated when postsecondary institutions apply the real-world test: Is a student ready for college work or a demanding training program?

Too often, the answer is no, which leads back to the sluggish progress we've seen in improving K–12 schools. Consider just one badly needed improvement: teacher quality. It doesn't take an education researcher to understand the importance of placing a high-quality teacher in every classroom. Any parent can tell you that, which is why so many parents angle to have their child placed with a teacher they have concluded is the best person to teach third grade, ninth-grade algebra, or whatever hovers just over the academic horizon. Yet progress toward upgrading teacher colleges, long known for failing to provide new teachers with the skills they need, has been minimal. Why is the Relay Graduate School of Education, featured in Chapter 5, among the lonely innovators? The answer, unfortunately, is that universities have little incentive to change what is accurately dubbed a "cash cow" — education students who pay full tuition but require few university investments.

And why is Teach For America one of the few lonely innovators in the area of recruiting more top-performing students into the teaching professions? The answer, unfortunately, is that most school districts run unimaginative recruiting operations that fail to discover new teacher pipelines. Most parents, especially those who live in urban areas where schools have sketchy achievement records, can barely imagine what a school staffed entirely with high-performing teachers would look like. We can, because we visited True North Troy Prep in Troy, N.Y., where every single teacher was trained in teaching techniques designed to reach all students — their students, the kids from low-income families who arrived at True North after enduring several years in traditional public schools that were mostly failing them. No visitor to True North leaves without saying to themselves: It's possible. The dream is achievable.

Why — when we know from 10 years of findings unearthed by the scrupulous investigations carried out by researchers working for the Broad Prize for Urban Education that a relentless use of data is the secret sauce used by the top-performing districts — do so many districts fail to use data to boost student learning?[8] Places such as Long Beach, Aldine Independent School District outside Houston, and Miami-Dade County Public Schools can track their students in near-real time. They know which schools and which teachers need extra help. Most important, they know which students need which lessons retaught. In Miami, Superintendent Alberto Carvalho ushered in DATA/COM, a school-scouring exercise inspired by successful data techniques pioneered in the New York City Police Department to reduce crime. Principals of struggling schools come to the ninth-floor conference room at the district's central office, where the superintendent and his team project all their data on a screen and pick it apart. Punishment is not the point of the exercise.

Rather, the entire group discusses what strategies and resources are required to correct the academic lapses the data unearth.

Why aren't more districts pushing harder to improve? The somewhat embarrassing truth is that too many districts and states have low academic ambitions for their own children. That sounds impossible, of course. Don't states have overpowering incentives to create educated workforces to compete both against other states and internationally? Yes, but the gravitational pull of the status quo appears to be equally strong. Why change when no one is complaining? Consider the story of Methuen High School detailed in Chapter 9, the only high school in this small city in northern Massachusetts. About a third of the students there are minority, mostly Latino, and a third are low income. For years, Methuen treated access to its AP courses in the typical manner, with students screened based on grades, essays, teacher recommendations, and interviews. Only the "best" were allowed in, which meant for 20 years the AP enrollment there never really grew. Only 74 students in this school of 1,900, roughly 4 percent, took an AP Exam in 2009. Then Morton Orlov II, a retired Army infantry officer who had taken over the Mass Math + Science Initiative, showed up and asked the staff to consider another way. The school's AP teachers bought into his plan to expand AP access and produced rapid results: Within two years, the enrollments in AP math, science, and English courses soared from 59 to 543, an 820 percent increase. The first year of the initiative produced 141 passing scores on AP Exams to qualify students for college credit; the second year, 167. The current goal: 226 qualifying scores by 2014. If successful change could come about that quickly, why had Methuen not acted earlier? The same reason a lot of schools never shift policy. The status quo prevails. Many parents don't see the problem because they've never known what great schools look like.

The schools, districts, and states we profile in this book have moved well beyond the status quo. The reasons behind their success in spreading rigorous course work fall into these key areas: leadership, innovation, equity, teacher quality, and parent engagement.

School Leadership

The successful schools we visited ranged from tiny charter schools to sprawling urban districts. What could classrooms at Rocketship's Mateo Sheedy Elementary School in San Jose have in common with the sprawling Hillsborough County Public Schools in Tampa? What could the tiny True North Troy Prep in chilly upstate New York, serving mostly African American students, possibly have in common with the schools in warm, sunny Long Beach, Calif., serving an ethnic mix of students ranging from Latino to Cambodian? The answer is not complicated: Each school has a unique culture of learning that comes from the top. In some cases, such as the successful school reforms in Maryland, the inspiration comes from the very top. In Chapter 12, we describe the work done by former State Superintendent Nancy Grasmick. In other instances, the inspiration arises at the principal's level.

As described in Chapter 1, a striking culture change played out at Houston's gritty Furr High School, where at age 66 Principal Bertie Simmons took over a high school ridden with gangs and infected by a cadre of teachers who didn't think their pupils had any academic potential. To the faculty, teaching was just a job, and a hopeless one at that. To the students, school was a place to park themselves. It took Simmons several years to pull it off, but anyone walking the hallways of Furr today has reason to feel hopeful about the future of urban education. How often does that happen?

In Long Beach, establishing a culture of learning took a village of leaders, including civic and business leaders who realized their fading shipyard and aircraft industries left them with only one certain hope for a brighter future: educating their students. Today, the Long Beach culture is a wonder to observe, with students in high-poverty neighborhoods producing test scores that rival those from cross-town schools that enroll middle-class students. How often does that happen?

At True North Troy Preparatory, the culture of learning gets passed down from Doug Lemov, whose book, *Teach Like a Champion: 49 Techniques that Put Students on the Path to College*, has turned into a phenomenon among teachers eager to put his exacting techniques into practice.[9] A visitor popping in on classes at True North can get a glimpse into teaching's future:

Powerful teaching can make an immediate difference in the lives of all students, including students from low-income families who have endured years of bad schooling before arriving there.

Some might be tempted to say that we have merely found inspirational figures, which triggers the oft-heard caution: Never count on finding enough charismatic leaders to take over struggling schools. To some extent, that's true. Bertie Simmons is a rare breed. But Chris Steinhauser, who leads the Long Beach schools, and MaryEllen Elia, the superintendent in Tampa, would never make it on Broadway playing school leaders. They are pleasant, soft-spoken, and earnest — not flashy. But they are long on vision. While still a teacher, Elia saw that her middle-class high school students came up short on literacy skills and pursued a second master's degree in reading education. She didn't need that degree to meet her district's salary "step requirements," but her students badly needed her to have the skills it gave her. Very long vision. Steinhauser is a master of releasing just the right instructional reform at just the right take-it-slow pace, making sure that all teachers are on board and thoroughly trained.

The pace at which a new culture can take hold in school, or in an entire district, appears to vary greatly. Clearly, it is easier to establish a great learning culture in a startup school. Principals at startup charters in Uncommon Schools (which includes True North) know exactly what kind of teachers they want to hire, exactly how to train them in the school culture, exactly how to hone their skills on a weekly basis. Plus, parents signing up for these schools agree to abide by the school's unique culture. By contrast, at Houston's Furr High, Simmons faced an uncooperative faculty she was not allowed to fire and a student body rife with gang problems. As a result, Simmons had to wait seven years before introducing the school's first college-preparatory classes, and even then most students fell short of earning college credit in those courses. In Long Beach, the slow-but-constant improvements might best be described as incremental, a scorned word among many school reformers who believe quick change is both possible and necessary. Spurning incremental change backfired on former Washington, D.C., Chancellor Michelle Rhee, who after taking office in June 2007 forced through multiple rapid reforms — firing incompetent central office workers, closing failing and underenrolled schools, firing teachers she found ineffective. By October 2010, she was forced to step down after the mayor who appointed her lost his job, in part because of the unpopularity of her fast-paced reforms.

Does Rhee's fate mean rapid culture shifts in traditional school districts are not possible? Not necessarily. The new Washington mayor, Vincent Gray, who as city council president was one of Rhee's biggest critics, not only retained her reforms but appointed Kaya Henderson, her deputy chancellor, to take her place. Houston Superintendent Terry Grier is pushing through school reforms every bit as radical as Rhee's — and surviving the backlash. At Grier's "Apollo 20" schools, he gives fresh-picked principals the freedom to take over failing schools and carry out charter school–style reforms such as longer instructional days and highly targeted tutoring. Lee High School Principal Xochitl (pronounced So-CHEE) Rodriguez-Davila took us on a tour through remarkably calm hallways. The year before she took over, the school was charitably described as a drop-in community center, with students doing what they pleased. The school wasn't just low performing, it was a mess. In Rodriguez-Davila's first year at Lee, she replaced 40 percent of the staff, and the changes continued the second year. "I look for teachers who are relentless, teachers who are never going to give up," Rodriguez-Davila said. "I'm more interested in the passion for teaching than skills. We can teach skills." Each teacher also got a copy of Lemov's book and some lessons on how to use his teaching techniques. At Lee, the success arising from the rapid reforms was seen even in the first-year test scores.[10]

Culture change, regardless of the pace, starts at the top.

Innovation

There's nothing really innovative about what Bertie Simmons did at Houston's Furr High School. Just old-fashioned love, an outsized personality, and a passionate persistence born of nearly eight decades of life filled with both triumphs and pains. Simmons learned dearly from both. In Long Beach and Tampa, you'll see innovations, but nothing that would set off fireworks. In those school districts, the formulas for success come down to block-and-tackling issues: Let's settle on one reading program and make sure it's taught to perfection. Let's come up with a system for recruiting the best and brightest and play that out every year like it's the Super Bowl. Let's assume that most students can handle a college-track curriculum and find ways to make sure they get on that course. Once you decide that poverty shouldn't entirely predict destiny, lots of questions get answered, quickly and correctly.

That doesn't mean that innovations don't matter. What Rocketship charter schools do in San Jose — and are poised to do on a far larger landscape — is striking. These schools give low-income Latino children an education that produces results rivaling those of their middle-class white and Asian peers. Few even dreamed it was possible. Rocketship's blended learning model, in which eventually the digitized Learning Lab will be the place where students learn their basics, is a highly promising work in progress. But that's not the only innovation at Rocketship. Less noticed is its success in turning its Latino parents into passionate school reformers. Rocketship destroys the stereotype that Latino parents shy away from passionate public engagement. Now there's an innovation.

In education, innovation is often thought of in terms of gadgets, such as interactive whiteboards utilizing touch-screen technology. Sure, whiteboards make blackboards look like horses and buggies, but the more significant innovations come in the creation and organization of new schools. The new wave of high-performing charters, such as KIPP (Knowledge Is Power Program), are supported by charter management organizations (CMOs) that have learned how to commoditize quality. Starting a new school is an extraordinarily difficult task — in many cases, it takes years to build a functioning learning culture. Schools launched by the top CMOs, however, often succeed in their first year.

Another innovation in reorganizing to help troubled schools was inspired by the success seen in New Orleans with the Recovery School District, a startup born of the devastation of Hurricane Katrina. What was once one of the worst urban school districts in the country is now flush with revitalized schools drawing visitors from around the country wanting to know, how did you make that happen? New Orleans has inspired special district launches in Tennessee and Michigan. Tennessee tapped Christopher Barbic, founder of the highly successful YES Prep Public Schools in Houston, to take over a special district that eventually will oversee the lowest 5 percent of schools in the state. "There's definitely skepticism, and honestly, I think there should be," Barbic told *Education Week*. "But I do think there's a healthy dose of optimism as well. We want to make sure that we're putting ourselves in a position to get results, and we want to do this slowly and methodically."[11] In Michigan, former Kansas City Superintendent John Covington is attempting the same. "They're still not there," Covington said of the New Orleans Recovery School District, "but if you look at where they are compared to where they started, it's almost mindboggling."[12]

The most important innovations may be arising from community colleges forced to step in to fix academic inadequacies borne by their incoming students. In theory, community colleges have no obligation to work with high school students. That's the job of K–12 schools, right? And states give them no financial incentives to fix what needs fixing. Yet some community colleges work with high schools anyway, assuming collective responsibility even though they don't share the blame. "The best community colleges recognize that there are limitations students are coming with, but don't use that as an excuse," said Joshua Wyner, executive director of the Aspen Institute's College Excellence Program. The Aspen Institute recently launched a national prize targeting community colleges with practices worth imitating.

Miami Dade College, profiled in Chapter 13, requires students forced to take remediation to simultaneously take a credit-bearing life skills class. "If you're juggling a full-time job, if you have financial challenges, if you don't know how to manage your time or how to take notes, it's the difference between staying in school and dropping out," Wyner said.

At innovative community colleges such as Miami Dade and Orlando's Valencia College, winner of the first Aspen prize, no one initiative emerges as a silver bullet guaranteed to reverse the remediation problem. Rather, these colleges create an elaborate weave of support that adds up to something intangible: an expectation that students will persist and earn degrees, regardless of their academic shortcomings upon arrival. Said Wyner: "Given where students are when they arrive, [colleges] have to ask, 'What can we do to help?' They simply will not allow what students arrive with to be an excuse for not serving them."

Equity

The Achievable Dream is about the pursuit of equity. It can happen because it is happening, at least in the schools we profile here. Following these lessons will make it spread. We have described efforts ranging from building high-quality preschools to overhauling college remediation. We are under no illusions that knowing what works makes the job easy. The lingering recession has not only exacerbated poverty rates, but also produced more high-poverty families in suburban areas not accustomed to dealing with such challenges. Between 2006 and 2010, the number of students receiving subsidized lunches rose from 18 million to 21 million, a 17 percent increase. Many states, including Florida, New Jersey, and Tennessee, saw four-year increases of 25 percent or more. Nearly a third of those families lived in the suburbs in 2010, an increase of 11 percent over the previous year.[13] In many areas, including Atlanta, Austin, Dallas, Indianapolis, and Milwaukee, the suburban poor population more than doubled between 2000 and 2010.[14]

Rising poverty rates make everything harder — but not impossible. In recent years, "poverty" has turned into a false debate, with critics of the school reform movement arguing that reformers ignore the overpowering role poverty plays in education. They have a point. Some reformers, especially those within the world of the high-performing charter schools, get carried away with their rhetoric. A child attending a KIPP charter school does not graduate with the same college readiness skills that most upper-middle-class students possess when graduating from suburban or private schools.[15] But is that really the debate? What is clear is that those KIPP graduates are far more likely to go on to college than their neighbors who went to regular public schools. As seen in Chapter 2, at least at the elementary level, a high-performing charter school serving an all-poor, all-Latino student population can produce outcomes that are nearly equal to those seen in middle-class schools. In Chapter 11, we profile an urban school district, California's Long Beach, where poor, minority students turn in better-than-predicted results that lead to strikingly better college-going rates.

When it comes to schooling, no reasonable person underestimates the destructive power of poverty. At the same time, no reasonable person — especially anyone who has visited a Rocketship charter or the Long Beach schools — can argue that waiting for poverty to be solved is a reason to maintain the status quo in urban school districts that are failing their students. The increasing poverty challenge only makes these school reform efforts more urgent.

One of the clearest examples of equity we saw was in Tampa's Leto High School, which is mostly Hispanic, with about 80 percent of the students qualifying for subsidized lunches. In a typical high school like Leto, the AP offerings would be slim. Many students wouldn't even know about them. Leto educators start preparing the students for college-track classes one or two years in advance, giving them a taste of what it takes to take on a rigorous course. Then, it is assumed students will take AP classes, regardless of the score earned on the 1-to-5 matrix. "A score of 1 or 2 only means that you are not ready for college credit," said Eric Bergholm, who oversees the district's effort to ramp up the number of students taking high-rigor classes. "That student still took the course and most likely received a decent grade and got the benefit of a rigorous curriculum. ... A score of 1 means you are ready for high school; you're rocking it. That's fine. They are in high school. A 2 is actually pretty good. That means you are perched to receive college credit."

Some critics argue that the aggressive practices at Leto end up watering down AP classes, thus hurting students who might have a shot at earning college credit. On the surface, that would seem to make sense. But in practice, that's not what happens: No district in the country has achieved a larger increase since 2008 than Hillsborough in the number of students earning AP Exam scores of 3 or higher for college credit.

Equity is what we saw playing out in Chapter 7, which profiles an AppleTree preschool in Washington, D.C. With its exacting curriculum, low teacher–student ratio and well-trained staff, AppleTree appears capable of infusing poor and minority children with the kindergarten-readiness skills that seem to come almost naturally to white and Asian middle-class students. "When the children arrive in kindergarten," said Lydia Carlis, director of education for AppleTree, "there's a huge difference between the children who learned 'bat' from rhyming and alliteration and those who learned how to break and rebuild the sounds. They don't need to be reading by the time they get to kindergarten, but they do need to have all of those foundational skills." That's equity.

Teacher Quality

Given what we know about the importance of having your child taught by a highly effective teacher, you might assume that by now educators would have figured out how to get effective teachers into the classrooms that most need them. They have not, and that is alarming. Poor kids whose parents haven't been to college should not have to face Vegas-like odds to win a shot at equity. Nearly every study of classroom staffing shows that schools serving these children rely heavily on ineffective teachers. Just take one indicator, the number of first-year teachers: High-minority schools have twice as many as low-minority schools.[16]

We urgently need to send the best teachers to the highest-needs classrooms, and school districts don't know how to make that happen. Some advocates want to offer substantial bonuses for teaching in more challenging schools. On paper, that's a winner. But in the real world, it's unclear how that can work on a scale big enough to make a true difference. True, teachers care about extra money, but perhaps not as much as they care about agreeable working conditions. Others want to force the more effective teachers to transfer to schools in greater need. Again, there are logistical challenges. If the working conditions aren't great at the transfer schools, those teachers might just quit.

Using improved teacher evaluations to fire (or counsel out) ineffective teachers is a tool that appears on the ascendancy, as more states mandate "real" teacher evaluations that are typically based in part on tests measuring whether students made academic progress. While teacher evaluations that actually measure teacher effectiveness represent the future, considerable challenges lurk in the short term. Many states are ushering in these evaluations with crude mechanics, leaving teachers wary of their reliability, and confusion reigns over how to use the information. Do you use evaluations to improve the effectiveness of teachers who need it the most? That sounds right, but professional development has never been an area in which schools have excelled. Do you use the evaluations to fire teachers unlikely to improve? In some cases, that must be done, but to date no school superintendents have shown they can fire their way to success. What about using the evaluations to reward the top performers? Those top performers certainly deserve better pay, but how does that help the students stuck with the less effective teachers? The answer, of course, is that school leaders will employ a mix of those strategies. Which brings us back to the need for great leaders capable of finding the right mix for their individual schools.

In researching this book, we found examples of entire school districts experiencing success in boosting teacher quality. On the surface, they appear to have taken different pathways to success. One district sends small teams of successful teachers into troubled schools. Another district partners with a local university to both train and recruit the best candidates. A charter school organization trains rookie teachers recruited by Teach For America.

Consider Charlotte-Mecklenburg schools. When Paul Gorman arrived as superintendent in 2006, he concluded that changing the "cycle of failure" in his struggling schools took more than a terrific principal; it required a team. Thus was born the "strategic staffing" initiative, in which principals who had proven they had the talent to turn around schools got to select five teachers who had proven the same. Together, they would sweep into a school and change the culture, partly by fiat from above, partly by inspiration. The strategy worked at all seven schools where Gorman tried it.[17] Teachers and administrators in those schools experienced success, and success became infectious.

Long Beach schools benefit from a partnership with Long Beach State University. District officials teach at the university — guaranteeing that would-be teachers understand the "Long Beach way" of instruction — and also keep a close watch on the best recruits. Once in the classroom, Long Beach teachers benefit from a complex system of professional development. New instructional initiatives first get teacher buy-in and are then delivered slowly so all teachers have a chance to become competent with the changes. All this earns Long Beach a uniquely competent corps of teachers, drawn there in part because they know about the district's success.

Rocketship hires almost exclusively from candidates already screened and trained by Teach For America. Those green teachers then enter a unique training program that makes most of them effective teachers during their first year on the job — a rarity. Thus, would-be teachers have two reasons to apply to Rocketship: They know their training and support will be first class, and they know they will be making a difference. Former

Colorado Springs Superintendent Mike Miles concluded that schools could benefit from the performance-based personnel systems he experienced in both the Army and Foreign Service. In only a few years, he steered Harrison School District Two to a place other school districts can only imagine: salary increases based on how well teachers are teaching. Several things are interesting about what Miles has accomplished, starting with the fact that his accomplishment came with far less turmoil than anyone might have predicted. Also surprising is that most teachers agree they have been correctly "placed" in the evaluation system. Even more interesting is the sorting that has taken place. Some teachers did get fired for performance reasons, but not as many as might have been predicted. For the most part, teachers sorted themselves out. Those who were uncomfortable with the new system found jobs elsewhere. Those interested in being rewarded for their effort and competence found their way to Colorado Springs and applied for jobs.

What's encouraging in the teacher-quality debate is the coming together of all sides — advocates, superintendents, and union leaders — to focus on that one issue. In December 2011, Teach For America founder and CEO Wendy Kopp teamed up with National Education Association President Dennis Van Roekel to develop a three-point plan for boosting teacher quality. They called for (1) more aggressive use of data to improve teacher preparation programs, long a weak link in the nation's teacher supply line, and (2) improved teacher professional development programs.

Kopp and Van Roekel's third call to action — bringing new talent into the field — may prove to be the most difficult goal to accomplish. Teach For America has succeeded in drawing in many of the nation's top graduates, but that's not enough. Although many TFA alums remain educators after their two-year commitment, many others treat it like a stint in the Peace Corps and move on to careers that draw more respect and compensation. Plus, many school districts, and the unions representing their teachers, still view TFA as an unwelcome interloper.

The real transformation in teaching will come when graduates of Harvard and Stanford apply not to TFA for two-year obligations but rather directly to individual school districts for true teaching careers. There's a huge pool of untapped talent here. In 2011, Teach For America had nearly 48,000 applicants for 5,000 teaching positions, including nearly 12 percent of all seniors at Ivy League schools, 10 percent of the graduating class at Howard University, 8 percent of seniors at the University of Michigan-Ann Arbor, and 5 percent of the graduating class at the University of Texas at Austin. And, at Ivy League schools, 1 in 5 African American seniors and 1 in 6 Latino seniors applied. In general, these are not students majoring in education and planning teaching careers. To date, they have trusted TFA, but not traditional school districts. But that could change.

That's how MaryEllen Elia in Tampa sees it. "At some point I want to be able to walk into Harvard and say, 'You can go to TFA or can come to Hillsborough County Public Schools,'" she said. Given her district's recent success and the new evaluation system unfolding that will compensate teachers based on performance, Elia feels she is close to making that dream a reality. "I think they are looking for that value of going in and helping people who are less fortunate," she said. "I can work with them. I can help them become successful."

Elia has it right. School districts with demonstrated success, good professional development, and a compensation system that makes it respectable to teach will draw the best and brightest. High-performing charter schools have proven they can draw teaching talent from this country's most elite colleges. Why not Hillsborough and other large urban school districts that are turning the corner?

Family Engagement that Engages

To state the obvious: Students with engaged parents do better in school, and nobody knows a child's academic needs better than his or her teacher. So basic, and yet scores of schools have wasted untold resources doing everything but pairing these two groups of people together. Most schools fail to define family engagement at all, much less define it in terms of working with families to improve student learning. This fuzziness leads to an untold number of hours wasted on bake sales, potlucks, newsletters, and too-short conferences at back-to-school nights. Where's the academic engagement? Some schools attempt to outsource family engagement to paid parent coordinators, but this often cuts out the teacher. Without academics in the conversation, what's the point?

In Creighton, Ariz., Maria Paredes built a parent engagement program that actually improves student outcomes (see Chapter 8). Her model lays out precise roles and expectations for teachers, students, and parents. Teachers share with parents easy-to-understand data about how students are doing compared with each other and against grade-level goals. Parents learn specific exercises to teach their children outside of the classroom. They set goals around what they will do to increase their children's performance, and by how much, and they're back in 60 days to see if it worked.

....

Jack Jennings, a veteran Congressional education staffer and founder of the respected Center on Education Policy, retired in January 2012. His parting gift was a revealing white paper looking back on 50 years of education reform. The title: *Why Have We Fallen Short and Where Do We Go From Here?* Jennings takes readers through the three major reform movements: equity (e.g., supplementing funding for poor schools and giving special protections for students with disabilities), school choice (e.g., vouchers, charters, and public school choice), and standards (best illustrated by the passage of No Child Left Behind). All three enjoyed broad support, and all three had an impact, he concludes. But not nearly enough. "The most noteworthy shortcoming of these movements is that they mostly sought to influence what went on in the classroom — the heart of education — through external means," Jennings wrote. To move forward, he says, schools need an internal focus on what is taught — and by whom. His conclusion matches ours. The work we are advocating will not be easy. As Jennings points out, raising teacher quality will require closing ineffective colleges of education, substantially increasing teacher pay, removing ineffective teachers, and somehow attracting the most talented teachers to the most challenging schools.

All those steps are expensive, controversial, or both. But we must take them, and not just because this is a civil rights issue. We must act because, as these chapters show, the dream is achievable. And if it is achievable, and the future of the county depends on realizing that dream, is there any choice other than taking action?

Endnotes

1. "Survey Finds Rising Perception of Class Tension," by Sabrina Tavernese. The New York Times. Jan. 11, 2012.

2. The Alliance for Excellent Education estimates that the approximately 1.2 million students who should have graduated with the Class of 2008 will cost the nation nearly $319 billion in lost income over the course of their lifetimes.

3. Community College Research Center research; Gates Foundation.

4. "$70M in Remedial Work for Unprepared Students Saps SUNY Budget," by Scott Waldman. Albany Times-Union. Feb. 1, 2012.

5. "Learning Denied: The Case for Equitable Access to Effective Teaching in California's Largest School District." The Education Trust-West. January 2012.

6. "Black, Latino Students Perform at Levels of 30 Years Ago," by Teresa Wiltz. America's Wire. Jan. 23, 2012.

7. Exact figures here are difficult to determine. According to one study cited by the Community College Research Center, 13 percent of college-ready community college students end up with a bachelor's degree in five years, compared with 2.5 percent of the students referred to developmental education. However, it would be expected that students having to enroll in remedial courses take longer to graduate.

8. The prize is sponsored by the Eli and Edythe Broad Foundation.

9. Jossey-Bass, 2010.

10. Some of the material about Lee High School first appeared in the article "Reason for Hope in Urban School Reform," by Richard Whitmire. Youth Today. Dec. 15, 2011.

11. "States Creating New Districts to Steer 'Turnarounds,'" by Christina A. Samuels. Education Week. Dec. 14, 2011.

12. Ibid.

13. "Lines Grow Long for Free School Meals, Thanks to Economy," by Sam Dillon. The New York Times. Nov. 29, 2011.

14. "Parsing U.S. Poverty at the Metropolitan Level." Brookings Institution. September 2011.

15. About a third of KIPP's middle school graduates, almost all of whom are minorities and come from low-income families, complete a four-year degree within 10 years. Among similar students who did not attend KIPP schools, roughly 8 percent graduate in that time period. "KIPP Schools: A Reform Triumph, or Disappointment," by Andrew Rotherham. Time. April 27, 2011.

16. Kati Haycock and Eric Hanushek, "An Effective Teacher in Every Classroom." Education Next. Summer 2010.

17. The reporting about Charlotte-Mecklenburg schools was done by Richard Whitmire for a research paper on lessons learned over 10 years from the Broad Prize for Urban Education. Charlotte-Mecklenburg schools won the prize in 2011.

ACKNOWLEDGMENTS

In mid-2011, as I was preparing to announce my retirement from the College Board, the time seemed right to share the many lessons I have learned over the years about what works in American public education — always focusing on the positive. The result was this book, *The Achievable Dream*, a story about the power of perseverance and optimism as much as a primer on successful tactics.

As I looked for a partner to work with me on the project, Richard Whitmire quickly jumped to the head of the line. Richard stood out for his depth of knowledge on education, his dedication to the issue, and his ability to break down complex ideas into digestible bites. Richard did the bulk of the writing, spending hours at my side as we labored to turn stories and experiences into accessible lessons.

Richard and I were able to draw on the impressive reporting and writing talents of former *Baltimore Sun* education reporter Sara Neufeld, who drafted several chapters, including those on teacher training, Maryland, and community colleges. Without Sara, we never could have produced a book of this quality on such a tight deadline. We also owe a debt of gratitude to Stand for Children — a nonprofit organization that mobilizes citizen activists who fight for real changes in public education — for allowing Tyler Whitmire (Richard's daughter) to write about her research on parental engagement.

There are also many people within the College Board who contributed to this book and deserve our thanks. Peter Kauffmann, who oversees communications for the College Board, acted as managing editor. Our internal publishing team, including Tylor Durand, Dian Lofton, Jennifer Rose, Anne Sussman, Bill Tully, and Karen Zeman, was integral to the design, photography, accuracy, and production of the piece. And there were many, many College Board policy experts and educators who contributed their knowledge and experience — too many to name them all, but they know who they are and they have our deepest thanks.

We also must thank the educators profiled in each chapter who spent valuable time discussing their work. They are too numerous to name here, so we express a blanket thanks to them all.

Finally, I would like to thank my parents, W.G. and Eliza Caperton, who always believed in me, particularly when it was difficult, and my sister, Cary Owen, who always set an example of excellence and commitment.

— Gaston Caperton

PHOTO CREDITS

Cover: ©2012 Victoria Jackson Photography

Chapter 1 – An Outstanding Principal: ©2012 Tom Callins

Chapter 2 – Visionary School Builders: ©2012 David Butow

Chapter 3 – An Exceptional Superintendent: ©2012 Gary Bogdon

Chapter 4 – Building Better Teachers: ©2012 Tom Sobolik

Chapter 5 – Overhauling Education Schools: ©2012 James Leynse

Chapter 6 – Boosting Teacher Quality: Courtesy of Harrison School District 2

Chapter 7 – The Preschool Potential: ©2012 Dennis Brack

Chapter 8 – Building Parental Involvement: ©2011 Steve Craft

Chapter 9 – Rising to the Challenge: ©2012 Rick Friedman

Chapter 10 – Urban Exam School: ©2012 Larry Evans

Chapter 11 – A Perpetually Improving District: ©2012 David Butow

Chapter 12 – A State Designed for Excellence:
    Portraits of Nancy Grasmick ©2012 Dennis Brack
    Portraits of Travana Eades ©2012 Greg Pease

Chapter 13 – Reworking Remediation: ©2012 Jeffery Salter

Assignment photography produced through Redux Plus, New York.